THE COMMUNICATION *MAJOR* FOR THE
UNDECIDED STUDENTS, THEIR CAREER
ADVISORS, AND TEACHERS: WHY STUDY
COMMUNICATION? Copyright © 2019 by the
Curious Academic Publishing.

ISBN: 978-1-925128-77-2
First Edition: 2019

Previously titled as "*Communication for the
Curious*", this book is part of the Interdisciplinary
Encyclopedia of Arts & Humanities Majors. If your
institution/organization needs bulk paperback
copies of this book or the hardcover encyclopedia,
please email: curious.publishing@gmail.com.

For a list of other books published by the Curious
Academic Publishing, please visit:
www.amazon.com/author/college

Disclaimer

This book is presented solely for educational purpose to provide information and motivation to our readers. It is distributed and sold with the understanding that the author, editor and publisher are not engaged to render any type of psychological, legal, or any other kind of professional services advice. The content of each article is the sole expression and opinions of its author, and not necessarily that of the editor of the publisher. While best efforts have been used in preparing this book, the author, editor and publisher make no representations or warranties of any kind and assume no liabilities of any kind with respect to the accuracy or completeness of the contents and specifically disclaim any implied warranties or merchantability or fitness of use for a particular purpose. Neither the author not the editor/publisher shall be held liable or responsible to any person or entity with respect to any loss or incidental or consequential damages caused, or alleged to have been caused, directly or indirectly, by the information or advice contained herein. No warranty may be created or extended by sales representatives or written sales materials. You should seek the services of a competent professional before choosing any major/minor, career, or undertaking any research/studies.

Dedication

This book is dedicated to all the curious students and readers – senior high school students (and their parents) who are considering Communication as their field of study, undergraduate students who are struggling to choose their major/minor, and graduate/research/PhD students who want to pursue further studies/research in the area of Communication.

Advisory and Editorial Board

Professor Even A. Culp, Ed.D
Professor Ronald Arnett, PhD
Professor Lisa M. Cuklanz, PhD
Gyromas Newman, PhD
Professor Abby Dress, APR
Associate Professor Kishor Vaidya, PhD
Professor Teri L. Varner, PhD

Table of Contents

Chapter 7: Why Study Communication? – Professor Kristina Horn Sheeler, PhD

What is Communication?

What is Communication Study as an Academic Discipline?

Career Opportunities for a Communication Major

Why Begin a Research Degree in Communication Studies?

Studying Communication at IUPUI

What is the Relationship between Academic and Applied Work?

Chapter 8: Communication & Rhetorical Studies: The Practical Liberal Art of the 21st-Century – Professor Ronald C. Arnett, PhD

21st-Century Study and Practice

Communication & Rhetorical Studies at Duquesne University

Applied Excellence

Recommendations

Interplay of Philosophy of Communication and Rhetoric

Research Foundation

An Energized Discipline

Chapter 9: Nothing So Practical as a Good Theory – Professor Maxwell McCombs, PhD

Many Messages Satisfy Curiosity - Few Make any Real Contribution

Theory is More than an Abstraction, More than just Ideas and Hypotheses

Agenda Setting Theory – an Example

Two Theoretical Roads

A Short Reading List

Chapter 10: An Important Part of your Education to Work in the Communication Field Happens Outside of the Classroom – Professor César García, PhD

Communication is a Perfect Field to Vehicle any Passion you may Have

How can Practitioners Benefit from Academic Research?

Benefits of Online Education

$80,000 for a Keynote Speech if you can Connect with the Business World!

Chapter 11: Communication Studies – Professor Richard Letteri, PhD

Preparing Students for Careers in Communication

Four Requirements of a Communication Major

Why the Communication Major is so Popular?
Summer Study Abroad and Other Programs
Research and Publications

Chapter 18: Why Study Public Relations and Social Media? – Abby Dress, APR

So you Want to Study Public Relations? What's That?
Growing in Reputation and Importance
Opportunities in Public Relations
Where Public Relations Students Fit
How Social Media Fares
Socially Correct to Audiences Directly
Public Relations Programs to Consider

Chapter 19 - Multiplatform Journalism: Purposes and Prospects – Professor Mike Dillon, PhD

Choosing Journalism as a Major: Role, Function, Knowledge, Skills
The Uses of Journalism Research
Academic Research and Journalism Practice
Best Practices: The Multiplatform Approach

Chapter 20: Intercollegiate Forensics and Mastering the Magic of Words – Professors Chad Kuyper, MFA; and Daniel Cronn-Mills, Ph.D

Why Study Communication

Preface

Given the investment in time and money that students will spend on higher education, understanding what they will learn in their chosen major and how it will prepare them for a career upon graduation is very important. As you read this book, we invite you to think about the types of skills that might be helpful for someone pursuing a career in Communication.

For students considering an undergraduate degree in Communication, this book has been prepared to assist you in your research of college majors by:

- Providing a description of Communication (which helps you understand what it is),
- Identifying courses typically found in this type of degree (which help you focus on what you will learn), and
- Discussing career opportunities in the field (which helps you understand why this degree is important for both you and perspective employers).

Additionally, this book will give you information and best practice advice on graduate/PhD studies and scholarships in Communication. If you are a practitioner/professional in Communication, you will find the discussion and insights from practitioner perspective interesting and helpful.

Whether you are a freshman/undergraduate student or graduate/PhD student or a practitioner, this book will give your lots of insights and best practice advice concerning the field of Communication. In this book, top professors from prestigious universities have answered answer the questions including:

- Why should you choose Communication as your major or minor?
- Why should you undertake a graduate/PhD degree in Communication?
- What are the research areas/issues and scholarship opportunities in field?
- What are the career options and best practice tips for the graduates?
- What are the academic/faculty peer-perspectives as to Communication education, research and practice?
- What are the key issues and best practices from the practitioner perspective?

A nine-member Advisory and Editorial Board was established as part of the publication/review process of this book. Most of the chapters in this book are peer-reviewed, and they have been written in plain English to give the best/easiest reading experience to the readers.

So, why study Communication – are you curious to know? You really need to read the book to find the answers but the following paragraphs provide a brief outline of each chapter.

"So You Want to Be a Communication Major? Opportunities in the 21st Century" is the title of **Chapter 1** from Professor Teri L. Varner of St. Edward's University. "Communication is an exciting, dynamic and fast evolving area of study and work and a degree in Communication gives students a wide range of employment options both in terms of the type of work they undertake and the industry sectors in which they can be employed", says Professor Varner. In this chapter, Professor Varner examines some of the challenges, opportunities, and advocacy concerns emanating from undergraduate students and affecting colleges and universities, Communication scholars, and students. He answers many questions such as concerns about the centrality of the Communication discipline, addresses the benefits of communication research and how effective forms of communication is an integral part of being a responsible citizen living in the 21st century. Professor informs you about the availability of various scholarships and offers you best practice tips based on his observation of Communication education, research and practice.

We have Professors Kevin Williams, Monica Larson, Jason McKahan, and Matt Kushin co-authoring **Chapter 2** entitled "**Computer-Mediated Communication: Creating Television, Film, Web-Design and Games While Socializing in the Global Village**". This chapter starts from a quote by Bill Gates. Professor Williams shares his childhood story to demonstrate the historical development of computer-mediated communication. "We are living in times of radical and rapid change. It is essential that we adapt so that we can excel in this environment. The study of communication prepares us to be highly skilled, creative, and employable in this electronic marketplace. However, it also prepares us to be highly educated, perceptive, and wise", the authors assert you. They talk about stories as the means of communication in greater details and suggest you to hone your storytelling skills. However, they also warn you to be cautious and to never take a story for granted as a communication student. They further suggest you that you need to ask critical questions: To whom are they communicating? What are their audiences' needs? What are the ultimate goals of these relationships? What are the strengths and weaknesses? This chapter is concluded with the discussion of power of computer-mediated communication in the age of social media.

"As business models change as the result of technological breakthroughs, so too does the workplace environment... This shift toward democratic work environments comes as classical leadership models are dying in the wake of celebration for individuality in the workplace", says Professor Brent Yergensen from Dixie State University in **Chapter 3** entitled "**the need for communicative wisdom in an age of workplace democracy**". In this chapter, Professor Yergensen discusses various issues including on the contemporary workplace and problem solving skills, strategic communication, the industrialized workplace, workplace democracy, teamwork, and presentation skills. "Success is driven and measured by the interactive craft and communicative wisdom creates and promises the longevity of a career", concludes Professor Yergensen.

Chapter 4 is on **the Communication Major** from Thomas Feeley of the University at Buffalo of the State University of New York. Professor Feeley argues that the Communication Major is a commonly misunderstood program of study despite its popularity as an undergraduate major and offers his perspectives from his experiences of teaching Communication at two universities. "Choosing Communication for entirely career-driven reasons is a mistake. To properly understand the field and communication processes, a student must dedicate herself to studying the history and theories of communication. Students should choose the Communication major if they are interested in studying the forms and potential influences in communication", suggests Professor Feeley. Why should you pursue a graduate degree in communication? What sort of scholarships and stipends are available? Why should you do a doctoral degree? Professor Feeley offers at least ten pieces of advice to you in this article. He has concluded this chapter by encouraging you to always ask "Why?"

What is the #1 competence the employers seek? If you rightly guessed, it is communication. In this **Chapter 5 ("Why Study Communication at the University of Nebraska-Lincoln?")**, Professor Dawn O. Braithwaite from the University of Nebraska-Lincoln discusses communication research issues including civic engagement, health and well-being, identify and difference, and translational scholarship. He also offers best practice advice to you. "Talk to as many professionals, within your field(s) of interest, as possible. Ask questions. Start networking. Do this sooner than later", says Professor Braithwaite. Professor Braithwaite concludes this chapter by advising you that you should work with passion, celebrate your achievements, but always hold an appetite for the greater challenges ahead. He has other pieces of advice to offer to you in this chapter. Why don't you "take a moment now and again to consider how you can turn everything on its ear"?

In **Chapter 6 (Communication is a Hot, Relevant, and Exciting Academic Discipline!)**, Professor Gary Kreps from George Mason University offers his personal perspective on the relevance of Communication education. What is the scope/future of the Communication discipline today? What is the demand for Communication graduates? Professor Kreps answers these questions for you in this chapter. He also highlights the value of Communication research and research training and shares his research programs examining health communication. So, how does academic research in Communication benefit practitioners? He answers this important question and offers recommendations for students and practitioners. "I want students to use what they learn to achieve personal and professional goals, as well as to help others effectively confront challenging issues...Through my teaching, I integrate theory, research, and practice", Professor Kreps concludes this chapter.

"Why Study Communication?" is the title of **Chapter 7** by Professor Kristina Sheeler of the Indiana University-Purdue University Indianapolis. Professor Sheeler answers some important questions for your information: What is Communication? What is Communication Study as an academic discipline? What is the relationship between academic and applied work? What career opportunities are available for a Communication major? Why begin a research degree in Communication studies? Professor Sheeler lists some key research questions for your consideration and shares her research interests with you. "All in all, the choice to study communication is a good one. Communication is a powerful process that helps to create stronger communities and better worlds', concludes Professor Sheeler.

In **Chapter 8** entitled **Communication & Rhetorical Studies: The Practical Liberal Art of the 21st-Century**, Professor Ronald C. Arnett of Duquesne University argues that communication is a practical liberal art. "Communication majors must learn why discourse shifts and changes from one context to another... A communication degree prepares our students to shape the future under conditions of uncertainty", says Professor Arnett. In this chapter, Professor Arnett discusses about Communication and Rhetorical Studies, its application in corporate communication, and offers recommendations. He talks about graduate and doctoral degrees in communication and points out several scholarship opportunities. "Indeed, there is no such thing as good communication. There is, however, a competent communicator in the 21st century. Such a person knows why knowledge matters in a given communicative setting and understands the persuasive character of the weight of such recognition and the consequence of testing ideas through thoughtful research", concludes Professor Arnett.

Nothing So Practical as a Good Theory is the title of **Chapter 9** by Maxwell McCombs of the University of Texas at Austin. "Millions of messages are created and distributed every day ...The central question about any message is whether it created awareness and understanding in the recipient. This is where the vast majority of the daily flood of messages falls short. Many messages satisfy curiosity. Few make any real contribution", says Professor McCombs. He highlights the importance of theory and argues that studying communication can create an understanding of the communication process that can be used personally as well as professionally. In this chapter, Professor McCombs discusses the agenda setting theory as an example. What are the two theoretical roads leading to theoretical advances in most fields of research? He answers this question and repeats that theory is more than just an intellectual tool. "Thinking theoretically can take you beyond the specific blueprints and enhance the effectiveness of your communications", concludes Professor McCombs.

Why should you choose Communication as your undergraduate or postgraduate major? What is the scope of this major in terms of career opportunities and options? Professor César García from Central Washington University answers these questions in **Chapter 10 (An Important Part of your Education to Work in the Communication Field Happens Outside of the Classroom)**. "In a noisy world where attention is even scarcer than money, catching a portion of attention through communication strategies and techniques have become a challenge for many organizations", says Professor García. Do you have any passion in life? In this Chapter, Professor García tells you that communication is a perfect field to vehicle any passion that you may have. Professor García also explains why a research degree is important and how a strong academic/scholarship background helps you in your professional career even if you do not want to become a university professor. "The professional world is looking for people who can identify and anticipate trends, among them communication trends that help to establish emotional connections with different audiences". Professor García concludes this interview with an example of Malcolm Gladwell who charges $80,000 per conference speech!

Professor Richard Letteri believes it is vital that students are aware of the principles, techniques, theories, and methodologies for the production and critical understanding of texts in the fields of rhetoric and mass communication. In this chapter entitled "**Communication Studies at Furman University**" (**Chapter 11**), Professor Letteri discusses the importance of public speaking and explains what you are expected/required to learn as a Communication student, and what opportunities including scholarships, internships, and stipends are available to develop your skills and understanding of communication. You might rightly ask, "How successful is this pedagogic strategy?" "Although we do not collect information regularly on our graduates, they have a very good track record in finding jobs shortly after graduation in a diverse set of fields", explains Professor Letteri.

Chapter 12 (An Internship or Practicum in the Industry is Critical) is the interview from Dr. Even Culp of the Oral Roberts University. What actually the academic major of Communication is? Why should you choose Communication as your undergraduate or postgraduate major? Why should you undertake a research degree in Communication? Dr Culp answers these questions and offers information on scholarships. He further shares his research interests including his doctoral research project with you and discusses research issues in this area of study. He also shares his perspective as to the most practical forms of research and communication. Dr Culp further shares his best practice tips on his observation on Communication education, research and practice with you and concludes this chapter with the discussion of his university's internship program.

Why Study Communication? In this interview (**Chapter 13**), Professor Alec Hosterman from Indiana University South Blend says it is a difficult question to answer. Why? Because... "You can do most anything you want with a degree in communication". "In fact, we study what people do at least 75% of the day. We speak and write well, think critically about the media we come in contact with, understand how people function in groups, prepare effective presentations, adapt to different situations, and more. And I guess this is why it is so difficult to answer why one should study communication", explains Professor Hosterman. What are the four abilities that students studying communication should excel at? Professor Hosterman answers this question and lists the skill areas that are popular among graduates in this digital age. Are you looking to pursue communication primarily as a research degree? If so, Professor Hosterman encourages you to think about two important things in this chapter. Are you interested in pursuing an education in communication? Professor Hosterman bleeds from his heart to offer timeless advice for you in this chapter.

In this brief chapter (**Chapter 14**), Professor David Hesmondhalgh of the University of Leeds offers **some thoughts on communication and media studies**. Professor Hesmondhalgh offers mixed prospects for communication and media studies as an academic discipline. "Many students understand its purpose in a particular way: as providing vocational training for people who wish to work in occupations such as journalism, public relations, advertising or even strange new jobs such as 'event planning'... But universities need to be about much more than vocational training" says Professor Hesmondhalgh. He believes that I believe that we can't understand the world without understanding communication and the media, and that everyone should study the communication and media at some point in their education, just as everyone should study literature, or art, or music, or history, if only for a little while. Can music be one of the forms of communication? Sure.

Professor Hesmondhalgh also shares his research interest in the area of music communication and discusses his work "Why Music Matters" in greater details. What are his messages to you? "Don't assume that knowing the newest developments is the most important thing; don't believe people who tell you that everything is changing, and that therefore everything that happened before the year 2000 (or whatever) is irrelevant; and look for wisdom as much as for information". Professor Hesmondhalgh concludes this chapter.

Communication as a Calling and a Career; the CU Denver Model of Civic Engagement is the title of **Chapter 15** by Professor Stephen J. Hartnett. "...Some of us like to joke that the Department of Communication should be called the department of democracy—for we see our mission as helping our students to work their ways into satisfying careers while also finding a calling, a passion, a project they can live with and grow with, all while contributing to the ethical, effective, and empowering debates that drive a healthy democracy", Professor Harnett starts this chapter. He explains in greater details as to the structure and objectives of the Communication major. I hope to have persuaded you to consider communication as your major, and to use your major as a springboard into the world of interdisciplinary learning and civic engagement. "With a degree in communication you can work for health care providers, international banks, various branches of government, community advocacy groups, any variety of media producers, advertising and marketing outfits, in both traditional and evolving forms of journalism, and hundreds of others", says Professor Harnett. He concludes this chapter by hoping that he has persuaded you to consider communication as your major, and to use your major as a springboard into the world of interdisciplinary learning and civic engagement.

What is Communication, and Why Should You Study It? In **Chapter 16,** Professor Gyromas Newman from the University of Mobile answers these questions in greater details. In this chapter, he asks you to think for a moment about what the world would be like without communication. - What if we could not share meaning between ourselves? "Not only would we not have our modern conveniences, we would not have society at all", declares Professor Newman. So, what jobs can you get with Communication major? "I'll usually answer with the typical laundry list of jobs for communication majors such as journalist, public relations practitioner, ad designer, writer, counselor, and so on. However, I often follow that list by remarking that a communication major will help you with any job that requires you to articulate

your own ideas and comprehend those of others",
answers Professor Newman. In this chapter,
Professor Newman also discusses about the
benefits of research to the students and also to the
practitioners. Why should you study
Communication? "Because communication has
such an impact on all of our lives, I counter the
question "Why should I study communication?"
with "Why shouldn't I?" To date, I've yet to think of
a good reason". Professor Newman concludes this
chapter with these thoughts.

Again, **Why Study Communication?** Professor
Lisa Cuklanz of the Boston College answers this
question in **Chapter 17**. In this chapter, Professor
Cuklanz discusses various issues including
communication coursework and internship
opportunities, the reasons for the popularity of the
Communication major, summer Study Abroad and
other programs, and research/publications. "The
field of Communication is relatively young in the
United States, and many of the oldest universities
and colleges do not have Communication
departments" notes Professor Cuklanz. Why is
Communication major so popular? According to
Professor Cuklanz, the combination of critical
thinking, theoretical frameworks, practical
knowledge, and relevance to the world outside of
the classroom all combine to make the major one of

the most popular on campus. "The increasing salience of communication processes, texts, technologies, and industries to our everyday functioning as individuals and as a society will likely mean that the field of Communication continues to expand and gain in popularity" Professor Cuklanz concludes this chapter.

So you want to study public relations? What's that? These are the questions from Professor Abby Dress from Long Island University in **Chapter 18** entitled **Why Study Public Relations and Social Media?** "Public relations has become a discipline in demand by business and other organizations. As a result, this has been a bonus to young females, particularly when they start families of their own. In fact, the field is an ideal career path for women (and minorities), who have become vice presidents, directors, partners or owners of their own businesses", notes Professor Dress. In this chapter, he also answers a number of questions for you including: What are the opportunities in public relations? How social media fares? What are the public relations programs to consider? Professor offers you a number of best practice suggestions and urges you to become fluent in a second language. "If you are interested in public relations or communications, then build your skills though a major or minor. There are lots of options and career paths that let you explore and grow", concludes Professor Dress. To read more about public relations and social media, please read the book *Public Relations and Social Media for the Curious* published by the Curious Academic Publishing.

Professor Mike Dillon of the Duquesne University has contributed **Chapter 19** entitled **Multiplatform Journalism: Purposes and Prospects**. In this chapter, Professor Dillon shades light on choosing Journalism as your major in terms of role, function, knowledge and skills. What do journalists do? "Journalists must sift through vast amounts of data, often controlled by agencies that do not want them to have it, weigh conflicting accounts from self-interested parties, draw connections between different kinds of information and then interpret and shape a narrative that is accurate, comprehensive and precise, and yet accessible to diverse publics who are awash in a sea of competing narratives – and they must do all this on deadline" explains Professor Dillon. Why should a student major in journalism to master the knowledge and skills if he or she might choose to work in a field outside of journalism? Professor Dillon asks you. According to Professor Dillon, the answer is simple: No other major teaches this distinct blend of skills, knowledge and communicative proficiency. In this chapter, he discusses the uses of Journalism research in terms of academic research and journalism practice. "I believe the future of media education in general, and journalism education in particular, lies with a multiplatform approach that facilitates convergence and encourages adaptability in a world of fast-changing technologies, platforms and revenue models" concludes Professor Dillon. If you want to read more about Journalism, you should read the book *Journalism for the Curious: Why Study Journalism* published by the Curious Academic Publishing.

Chapter 20 by Professors Chad Kuyper (Florida State College at Jacksonville) and Daniel Cronn-Mills (Minnesota State University, Mankato) is entitled as **Intercollegiate Forensics and Mastering the Magic of Words. Why take the time, effort, and energy to complete in inter-collegiate forensics?** "Forensics gives you so much. In our humble opinion, forensics is one of the best activities in college. And no matter your major, forensics will make you a better student, a better professional in your career, and a better citizen of the world" Professors Kuyper and Cronn-Mills answer their question. They hope you've enjoyed your brief trip through the magical halls of forensics and want you to "remember, to watch the skies"." An owl will soon deliver your invitation to the Forensics School of Wordcraft and Wizardry.

Time to practice your magic!", Professors Kuyper and Cronn-Mills conclude this chapter.

Some Thoughts about Studying Communication is the title of **Chapter 21** by Ronald Rice of the University of California, Santa Barbara. We know that the scope of Communication is very broad but what does it cover? Where to find resources in this field of study? Why do you need to study Communication? What are the possible Communication careers? Professor Rice answers these questions in greater details and asserts you that he personally maintains six important teaching principles in individual advising, undergraduate courses, and graduate courses. What are the principles and how does Professor Rice maintain them? Professor Rice explains them in this chapter.

Now about this book itself. This is the first book of its kind ever published on Communication education, research and practice. In this book, we have invited a number of Professors from top-ranked universities to share their perspectives and advice on Communication to help you.

At the Curious Academic Publishing, we have worked hard to bring the book/s of your interest in plain English. Please search your intended/current discipline on Google or Amazon for other books from the Curious Academic Publishing.

If you purchased this book through an online retailer such as Amazon and liked it, please leave an honest review (as to why you liked it). We would be really grateful if you shared your comments on the social media.

We, at the Curious Academic Publishing, hope you benefit from this book. Whether it's about making an informed decision about your major/minor or career options, or keeping yourself updated about the research trends/scholarship opportunities, this book will prove to be a valuable resource.

We wish you happy reading and all the best with your studies, research, and career in Communication.

K. Vaida, PhD
Editor-in-Chief
The Curious Academic Publishing

Chapter 1: So You Want to Be a Communication Major? Opportunities in the 21st Century- Professor Teri Varner, PhD

Dr. Teri L. Varner is an Associate Professor and Chair, of the Communication Department at St. Edward's University (Austin, TX). She is one of the first African American women in the nation to lead a Department of Communication. She holds a Ph.D. in Communication with an emphasis in Performance Studies from the University of Texas at Austin. She teaches basic courses in communication, communication theory, nonverbal communication, public speaking and listening. Her ethnographic qualitative research interests range from women of color in American higher education to hair/body politics to increasing the amount of classroom instruction devoted to teaching students how to actively listen in the 21st century. She has over 15 years of diversified experience in higher education including classroom instruction, directing, lecturing and coaching with an emphasis on communication skills enhancement, and oral interpretation. She has more than eight years of performing, directing, adapting poetry, prose, non-fiction and theatrical projects. She is highly skilled in editing and writing academic research and presenting both written and performance based scholarly presentations at national conventions. Dr. Varner is an active member of National Communication Association (NCA) and is currently serving on the International Listening Association (ILA) Nomination Committee. Her latest project examining the narratives of adolescent and young adult (AYAs) living with cancer and their perspective on listening and healthcare professionals will be presented at the European Listening and Healthcare conference, Nijmegen, The Netherlands on October 30 and 31, 2014.

Purposeful Curricular Pathways

One hundred years ago, teachers of public speaking broke away from the National Council of Teachers of English to establish the National Association of Academic Teachers of Public Speaking. 2014 marks the 100th anniversary of the founding of the National Communication Association (NCA). With nearly 7,500 members, NCA is the oldest and largest national professional communication association in the world. Researchers, educators, and professionals, work to understand and better all forms of human communication. More than 6,000 communication professionals participate in over 1,200 educational sessions at NCA's largest educational and networking event of the year.

The centennial is a time to celebrate the resilience of our place in the intellectual world. It is also a prompt for us to reexamine, to seriously engage with what we take to be "the past(s)" of both the Association and the now vast intellectual field comprising Communication Studies. As NCA prepares to welcome members and guests for the historic conference, this chapter examines some of the challenges, opportunities, and advocacy concerns emanating from undergraduate students and affecting colleges and universities, Communication scholars, and students.

Background and Introduction

Never before has college learning been more important to students or society. While college once was seen as elective for most Americans, today postsecondary study has become necessary preparation for career success and for navigating the complexities of a modern, innovation-fueled, global society. Yet, paradoxically, we also live in a new era of anxiety about whether college is really "worth it" and, increasingly, of new pressure to make visible the "value" of college learning. The ultimate key to students' educational accomplishment is, of course, the standards that faculty set for their own educational programs (Schneider, 2013).

Academic disciplines in higher education are routinely called upon to explain and justify their role in the educational enterprise. Some academic fields such as history and philosophy are more central in the pursuits of liberal arts, while others such as business administration and engineering are more related to career development. The discipline of communication is fairly unique as it crosses these boundaries (Morreale/Osborn, Pearson, 2000).

Many people ask why a student would choose to study Communication – what are the benefits? What does a degree in Communication 'give' you? What can you do with a Communication degree? What good jobs can you get with a Communication degree? Of course, the answers vary. Communication, like other Humanities degrees, is often seen as a luxury "that employment-minded students can ill afford" (New York Times June 18, 2013). Like many others, I would argue that formal training in effective forms of communication is an integral part of being a responsible citizen living in the 21st century.

Communication is at the core of human behavior,

allowing us to explore and learn about other cultures, strengthen social ties, create business and personal relationships, and facilitate exchange of information. In the fabric of learning, knowing, and expression, communication represents the thread that runs throughout, crossing borders, making connections, and drawing attention to correspondence (Gaston, 2013). In other words, with a degree in Communication your opportunities are infinite.

Almost no one questions the importance of our discipline. It is widely known that communication skills (e.g. written and oral) are highly valued in new employees. In fact, survey after survey shows that communication knowledge and skill (including specific domains such as interpersonal skills, group decision-making, leadership, and persuasion) are top qualities employers seek in new hires. Communication is often valued even above job-specific skills[i]. Communication skills are ranked FIRST among a job candidate's "must have" skills and qualities, according to a 2010 survey conducted by the National Association of Colleges and Employers.

This finding is robust across professions and over time (Hess, 2013). One thing I know for certain is this: communicating effectively will always be a central driving force for innovation and progress. Communication is an exciting, dynamic and fast evolving area of study and work and a degree in Communication gives students a wide range of employment options both in terms of the type of work they undertake and the industry sectors in which they can be employed. Human communication is inescapable.

Communication is one of the oldest disciplines, relying on rhetorical principles that date back over 2,000 years. Communication is also one of the newest academic fields of study. Majors in Communication Studies choose careers in a wide-variety of fields, including: management, sales, public relations, advertising, marketing, broadcasting, teaching, law, human resources, training, lobbying, labor negotiations, mediation, event planning, fund raising, campaign management, as well as many others. Competence in oral communication - in speaking and listening - is prerequisite to students' academic, personal, and professional success in life (Morreale/Osborn, Pearson, 2000).

Regardless of whether your earn your diploma from the University of Canberra in Australia or St. Edward's University in Austin, Texas – the decision to study this dynamic field is up to YOU! Regardless of your major – the Millennial

Generation have their work cut out for them. You will be expected to be prepared when you show up for class, be fully present, follow instructions, pay attention to details, complete assignments in a timely fashion, multi-task, listen with both ears and your heart; and, speak responsibly as you make the world a better place.

Research Areas in Communication

In recent years, SEU has made a commitment to constructing new facilities across campus, which has been of a particular benefit to the School of Natural Sciences. The John Brooks Williams Natural Sciences Center – North Building, a 65,000-square-foot facility, opened in Fall 2006. SEU recently broke ground on the second phase of science complex, the John Brooks Williams Natural Sciences Center – South Building, which is scheduled to open prior to the fall of 2013. This enhanced a priority of the university to increase scientific literacy.

For example, in 2012 - I teamed up with Assistant Professor of Physics, Paul Walter, Ph.D., to write a grant, "Presentational Speaking for Scientists (PSS)." At a time when 97% of publishing climate scientists are convinced that humans are at least partly responsible for climate change while less than sixty percent of the public feels the same way, getting the message across is key (Doran & Zimmerman, 2009).

Recently, National Communication Association (NCA) members, with some support from the National Science Foundation, brought a cohort of communication scholars to the American Meteorological Society (AMS) Annual Meeting in Seattle. For six days, some 20 scholars – some quite experienced, others entry level – took time to meet with each other and with AMS members to dialogue on risk communication, climate change messaging, social networking, communication of uncertainty, and many other topics.

One of the primary concerns needing to be addressed was how to get scientists to be more communicative because as senior policy fellow at the American Meteorological Society William H. Hooke (2011, p. 2) succinctly wrote, "Earth Scientists – climatologists, meteorologists, oceanographers, and the rest of my crowd – have trouble communicating." The PSS project strives to meet this challenge on a broader scale by enabling students majoring in any of the sciences to become effective communicators.

Given that science scholars from various cross-disciplinary studies all seem to advocate the need to build a stronger union between two historical opposing academic traditions: the sciences and the humanities. We, here at St. Edward's University are attempting to meet the demands from future employers such as *Chief Executive Officer and board member of CONNECT* - Duane J. Roth (2012) by creating scientifically literate citizens.

When responding to the question, "What should student be studying 10 years from now?" Roth expressed his need for *"a new major that prepares the future workforce for constant change by teaching broad-based knowledge in many disciplines. This major would consist of, among other disciplines, the basics of engineering, biology, chemistry, physics, law, business, humanities and communications..."* and be better prepared because 10 years from now the *"rate of change will demand workers who can easily recognize and accept the rapid evolution of science and technology."* Clearly oral communication discourse is of critical importance in the intensively fast-paced world of the 21st century. Science majors with a strong background in oral communication skills ultimately benefits everyone. Improving the communication abilities of future scientists through formal instruction in a variety of speech styles and purposes is a priority that St Edward's University is actively pursuing.

Scholarship Available for Domestic and International Students

St. Edward's University recognizes the hard work and high achievement of top-performing students. We consider your previous academic curriculum in addition to a standout essay and application. We offer academic scholarships to transfer students with outstanding academic records. We also offer academic and athletic scholarships for international freshmen and athletic scholarships for international transfer students. Academic scholarships require no additional application beyond your application for admission. The full-tuition Moreau Scholarship requires a separate application.

In addition to scholarships awarded by St. Edward's University, there are many scholarship opportunities available from outside sources. For more information check out: http://www.stedwards.edu/admission/internation al/scholarships.

What are your own Research Interests?

For years, college professors have said that oral communication is one of the most important skills

needed for success in postsecondary education –
and that too few entering freshmen display oral
communication   competency
(Rothman/Spectra/2013). Forty-six states and the
District of Columbia have adopted new standards
for all students in elementary and secondary
education. The Common Core State Standards are
explicitly designed to lay out the knowledge and
skills. The standards place a strong emphasis on
speaking and listening, including those abilities as
one of four key strands in English language arts.

Indeed, listening is an important part of the
communication process, yet there is a tremendous
lack of skill and training in this area. Most students
enrolled in introductory communication classes are
exposed to a single chapter on the most frequent
type of communication - listening. Basic
communication courses devote approximately 7%
to listening skills (Beall, Gill-Rosier, Tate, Matten,
2008).

Most schools offer some listening instruction in the
basic public speaking course, and less than 50% of
this time is devoted to skill development (Perkins,
1994). It appears that the majority of people would
much rather be talking than listening. In the K-12
classroom, the state of listening in education can be
grouped into four main categories of research

including listening elicitation, listening benefits listening education in the classroom, and listening education (Beall, Gill-Rosier, Tate, Matten, 2008).

Most listening continues to be taught as a unit in another course and any listening instruction is found in speech or public speaking communication courses. In fact, data from as recent as 2012-2013 reveal that there were 181 undergraduate courses in listening offered at educational institutions in the United States [*135 were at 4-year colleges; 46 at 2-year colleges*]. These numbers are up from last year, when there were just 157 undergraduate courses in listening. This 15% increase in a year is significant especially, when you take into consideration that there are 7,711 degree-granting institutions in the United States. [Source: *Market Data Retrieval's 2012/2013 catalog*]. This is perhaps one of the most interesting research findings to me as an Associate Professor of Communication.

My primary research interests include teaching active listening in the classroom as well as health communication. My typical teaching rotation of communication courses such as: Introduction to Communication, Presentational Speaking, Introduction to Performance Ethnography, Communication Theory, Nonverbal Communication, Active Listening, Special Topics in

Communication and Internship for the Communication Major. Clearly, several areas of scholarly interest to me are: listening, nonverbal communication, presentational speaking and health communication.

My most recent research interest is in the area of listening. In fact, the abstracts of my undergraduate upper level students were published in the Listening Post – a newsletter of ILA. See Listening Research (pp.12-16); Issue 110, April 2013. Furthermore, I presented in Washington, D.C. at the National Communication Association (NCA) 99th Annual Convention. The topic for the panel was: Teaching Listening: CONNections & Undergraduate Courses. This panel (1) examines how educators can address listening and learning style differences in the classroom (2) offers best classroom practices that gain and maintain student attention while also (3) increasing student comprehension.

Currently, I am conducting a research study that includes interviewing young adolescent teenagers living with cancer and collecting their stories about listening and healthcare. Adolescents and young adults (AYAs) face profoundly different medical and personal challenges than pediatric and older adult patients. I have been invited to present my results and experiences of AYAs with doctors, healthcare professionals, and healthcare entrepreneurs for an up-coming European Listening and Healthcare conference, Nijmegen, The Netherlands on October 30 and 31, 2014.

Why is Academic Research in Communication Beneficial to Student?

There are some practitioners that generally are less interested in taking advantage of academic research in communication because research (Miller and Seldin, 2014) suggests that supervision of a graduate study or an undergraduate honors program are viewed as less significant by deans in evaluating faculty performance. This unfortunately, could put programs such as *Lambda Pi Eta*[ii], McNair Scholars[iii], and CAMP[iv] at risk.

Fortunately, there are also practitioners that are more interested in taking advantage of academic research in communication. Researchers (Miller and Seldin, 2014) have found that, "In comparing the evaluation practices of overall faculty performance in 2000 with those in 2010, three significant trends emerged: (1) academic deans are almost unanimous in citing classroom performance as the most important index of faculty performance; (2) research, publication, campus committee work, and student advising have sharply gained in importance; and (3) length of service in rank is considered important, but has lost ground." The fact that research publication is ranked as the second most important hallmark of faculty performance speaks for itself.

Innovative technologies have dispersed 21st-century education into a variety of contexts outside the classroom. Because communication processes sometimes function differently in technological environments, we welcome research that investigates the role of communication in online course distribution, web-based training, social networking, information distribution systems, and other technology-supported contexts where communication accompanies or enables learning (Witt, 2012). As a human social scientist with a doctorate degree in Communication/Performance Studies as a concentration I suppose remaining objective or somewhere in the middle is beneficial.

How can Communication Research be more Relevant, Useful and Interesting to Practitioners?

Look around at our current environment and state of daily affairs. Indeed, there is a great deal of social media and the strong presence of ubiquitous technology. Now, I challenge you to think about themes that emerge. Does the primary subject matter - your research appeal to a wide audience? Does it have intrinsic value that will have mainstream cross-over appeal?

If yes, then how well can you give the conclusions of your research and have large audiences/mass media find it useful? I would offer that human connectivity is at the core of many respected Communication theories. I find it useful to remember that the "relevancy" of our discipline resides in the weight given to the number of published research and paper presented at professional conferences. Producing quality scholarship that is used and respected outside continues to be a driving force.

For example, Macke, F. J. (1991), begins with a study of communication as a field concerned with matters of oral performance. As the field progressed, according to Macke, the emphasis shifted toward the influence of social science, and finally the discipline has evolved into one that concerns the importance of language, ideologies, and communication technologies. McCloskey, D. (1994), Professor of Economics at the University of Iowa, argues that speech or "talk" has become central to interdisciplinary research and that the communication field has become one of the most pragmatic fields of study in academia.

McCloskey presents three basic premises to support this claim: a nation of new minorities needs better communication; we are living in a communications revolution comparable to the invention of printing; and, many people now earn their living from talk. McCloskey concludes that communication studies are central to interdisciplinary research and teaching.

Since the turn of the 21st century, the number of Black females entering doctoral programs—and ultimately, the professoriate—has been steadily on the rise Black women are attaining doctoral degrees at the highest levels in history and currently have the largest faculty presence of all women of color (Ryu, 2010). Scholars (Jones, et. all, 2013) have pointed out, "For Black women, multiple identities, including race and gender, intersect in ways that need acknowledgement during the socialization process." Interestingly enough, I am one of the first African American women in the nation to lead a Department of Communication. Black women faculty is becoming increasingly significant in the new millennium. I am collecting qualitative and quantitative research on listening styles of African American females – hoping to establish a Varner theory of Listening.

Having your scholarly research published and cited in peer-reviewed journals is a high honor but is also a very difficult and tedious process. As Stephanie Y. Evans (2007) points out, "Writing by faculty of color offers inside perspectives on difficulties these faculty members face daily. For example, Journey to the Ph.D.: The Majority in the Minority presents research by faculty and graduate students that highlights daily battles, while research provides histories of desegregation and ongoing demographic struggles in vastly different locations (Texas, University of Missouri and University of Michigan, respectively).

In the United States, today's racism is not the same as the overt racism of the past 1960s. The way that people of color are put behind now is mainly by a general failure to help. Assistance does not require handling people with kid gloves; it simply means taking work and scholarship by faculty of color seriously enough to challenge and support scholarship in a way that presupposes the possibility of success.

Best Practice Tips

The communication discipline is an essential component of the educational enterprise – from preschool to adult education. The field is particularly important in the arena of higher education. The results of the studies reported herein clearly indicate that communication education develops the whole person, improves the work of education, advances the interests of society, bridges cultural differences, and advances careers and the work of business. That being the case, it is essential that communication curricula should be led and taught by specialists trained in the discipline and in departments that are dedicated to the study of communication.

As a researcher with a strong interest in how communication can facilitate teaching, learning and research, I spend a lot of time thinking about my experiences with students and talking with colleagues about theirs. While most of our interactions in the classroom are positive, many students are increasingly difficult to engage, dismissive, or even disrespectful of the professoriate's role in their education. Students today face an incredibly large number of distractions from their course work, compared with the early 1980s or even the 1990s. Numerous factors compete for students' attention and require a strong work ethic in the classroom. What you really need to know about Communication is that you have infinite choices.

For me, I have always felt that communication

education is necessary and is one of the primary reasons that I am proud to identify as a Communication professor. It also explains why teach in this discipline. I employ students to work on being an A.C.E. This acronym stands for Achieving Communication Excellence (ACE). This is another catch phrase I have coined while at St. Edward's University. I use it most often in my COMM 1317: Presentational Speaking Class. I try to incorporate witty humor to overcome performance anxiety. After all, they are required to deliver four formal speeches in that class.

I motivate my students to develop enthusiasm for a discipline, to understand its complexities and to appreciate it both as a science and as an art. I see myself more as a facilitator than a disseminator of knowledge. My overall style also incorporates participation and methods of discovery. My passion for teaching comes from many sources: pride in my skill, belief that information is valuable, an opportunity for me to take the material to a deeper place and watching my students grow. I do what I can to also entertain as I also educate. So far, the students continue to enjoy my courses.

I have learned that students tend to respond more positively to instructors who listen to them, are calm and anxiety-free, and value their presence. *Communication Studies* is an ideal major for students with multiple interests and diverse talents. So if you want to be a Communication Major in the 21st Century, know that the opportunities are endless.

REFERENCES

Beall, M. L., Gill-Rosier, J., Matten, A., Tate, J. (2008). State of the context: Listening in education. *International Journal of Listening, 22,* 123- 132.

Doran, P. T., & Zimmerman, M. K. (2009). Examining the Scientific Consensus on Climate Change. *American Geophysical Union, 90*(3), 22- 23., http://dx.doi.org/10.1029/2009EO030002.

Evans, S. Y. (2007). Women of color in American higher education. *Thought & Action*, 131.

Gaston, P. L., Ph.D. (2013, September). The Thread in The Fabric. *Spectra, 49*(3), 10-13.

Hess, J. A. (2013, May). The Risks and Rewards of Serving As A Department Chair. *Spectra, 49*(2), 8- 11.

Hooke, W. H. (2011, November). Communication Researchers as Pygmalion: Turning Earth Scientists into Sparkling Conversationalists. *Spectra, 47*(4), 2-6.

Jones, T. B., Wilder, J., & La'Tara Osborne-Lampkin. (2013). Employing a Black feminist approach to doctoral advising: Preparing Black women for the professoriate. *The Journal of Negro Education, 82*(3), 326-338.

Macke, F. J. (1991). Communication left speechless: A critical examination of the evolution of speech communication as an academic discipline. *Communication Education,* 40, 125-143

McCloskey, D. (1994). The neglected economics of talk. *Planning for Higher Education,* 22, 11-16.

Miller, J. E., & Seldin, P. (2014, May). Changing Practices in Faculty Evaluation. *ACADEME, 100*(3), 35-38. pg. 37.

Morreale, S. P., Osborn, M. M., & Pearson, J. C. (2000). Why communication is important: A rationale for the centrality of the study of communication. *JACA-ANNANDALE-*, (1), 1-25.

Morreale, S. P., & Pearson, J. C. (2008). Why

Communication Education is Important: The
Centrality of the Discipline in the 21st Century.
Communication Education, *57*(2), 224-240.
http://dx.doi.org/10.1080/03634520701861713

Roth, D. J. (2012, January 18). Marrying the
Humanities and the Sciences. Retrieved July 23,
2014, from Xconomist Report website:
http://www.xconomy.com/san-
diego/2012/01/18/marrying-the-humanities-and-
the-sciences/

Ryu, M. (2010) Minorities in Higher Education:
Twenty-fourth Status Report. American Council on
Education.

Schneider, C. G. (2013). "Taking the Lead On The
Value of College," Spectra
(http://www.natcom.org/uploadedFiles/Publicatio
ns/Spectra/NCA_Spectra_2013_49_4_Final.pdf),
November, 9-14.

Schuessler, J. (2013, June 18). Humanities
Committee Sounds an Alarm. Retrieved from The
New York Times website:
http://www.nytimes.com/2013/06/19/arts/human
ities-committee-sounds-an-alarm.html.

St. Edward's University. (2014). Retrieved July 23,

2014, from U.S. News website: http://colleges.usnews.rankingsandreviews.com/best-colleges/st-edwards-university-3621.

Witt, P. L. (2012). The Future of Communication Education. *Communication Education*, *61*(1), 1-3. http://dx.doi.org/0.1080/03634523.2012.645391.

Chapter 2: Computer-Mediated Communication: Creating Television, Film, Web-Design and Games While Socializing in the Global Village – Professors Kevin Williams, PhD; Monica Larson, PhD; Jason McKahan, PhD; and Matt Kushin; PhD

Professor Williams received a BA in Communication and Fine Arts. His undergraduate studies merged music composition and performance, audio and video recording, and passion for the fine arts. After studying Ethnomusicology at UCLA for a brief time, he turned his attention to communication theory. He received an MA in Communication from William Paterson University, N.J., and a PhD in the Philosophy of Education from Ohio University, OH. He's published several books and papers, and numerous conference presentations based on Critical/Cultural and Phenomenological philosophy. His work on visual communication and embodiment won NCA's Visual Communication Division's Top Paper award in 2005. He is currently a Professor of Communication at Shepherd University, W.V.. He teaches courses in both media criticism and media production. The Communication Department at Shepherd University has built a program of Computer-Mediated Communication. With courses in music video, graphic novel, social media and digital filmmaking, the program integrates an artistic sensitivity with technological applicability. profkevinwilliams.com; kwilliam@shepherd.edu. The faculty of the Communication & New Media program, Department of Communications, School of Arts and Humanities at Shepherd University, WV, US, are building a center for the production and study of computer-mediated communication at the apex of the Baltimore, Washington DC Technology corridor. Our vision includes co-inventing and co-producing works such as this paper. Such intellectual integration is passed to our students in our production to publication program which seeks to bring upper-level student work to publication across the new media mindscape.

Monica Larson is an Assistant Professor in the Department of Communication at Shepherd University where she has been a faculty member since 2005. She completed her MFA at Academy of Art University and her BFA at Syracuse University. Prior to teaching at Shepherd, Larson was an entrepreneur, founding and serving as the creative force behind three high-tech companies, including one of the earliest web development firms in the country, a video game software company, and an online exchange for the financial services industry. Preceding her entrepreneurial efforts Larson worked for a nationally-awarded design and advertising agency. A reflection of her diverse background, Larson teaches a wide variety of courses covering Advertising, Game Design, Graphic Novels and Motion Graphics. Her research focuses on pedagogy and the integration of technology to support Comm-centric storytelling.

Dr Jason Grant McKahan is Associate Professor of Communication and New Media at Shepherd University. His major research interests are television and film production and studies, production history, adaptation, political economy, discourse analysis, and critical theory. His publications include articles and chapters (e.g. Jump Cut, Projections, SUNY Press) and contributions to literature on film propaganda (Holocaust Film Sourcebook [Preager, 2004], Monsters In and Among Us [Fairleigh Dickinson, 2007], Hollywood Counterterrorism [Proquest Dissertation]).

Matthew J. Kushin, Ph.D. is an assistant professor in the Department of Communication at Shepherd

University. He earned his Ph.D. from the Edward R. Murrow College of Communication at Washington State University. His research examines the role of online and social media in political and civic decision-making, expression, and participation. Classes he teaches or has taught include: Social Media, Politics & Social Media, Principles of Public Relations, Communication Theories, Communication Research Methods, (applied) Communication Research, Communication & New Media, Writing Across Platforms, Introduction to Mass Communication, Public Speaking, New Communication Technology.

The "Truth" about Computer-mediated Communication

"I think it's fair to say that personal computers have become the most empowering tool we've ever created. They're tools of communication, they're tools of creativity, and they can be shaped by their user" (Bill Gates).

I grew up aware that I was living in the age of communication. I was fortunate. I had parents who saw the future — and it was computers. We bought an Atari 800 from Sears the night they went on sale. These were the first readily available computers on the market. It was a dull grey box that did nothing until you fed it a series of floppy disks (DOS). Then, it could become anything you wanted. Well, to be honest, you could do only three or four things: word processing (although computers and dot matrix printers were considered cheating by schools!), spreadsheets and games were most prevalent. Of course, we played games, and learned how to hack code.

One night after dinner, my friend's father called us into the kitchen where the home telephone was mounted on, and tethered to, the wall. He dialed up the mainframe computer at Bell Labs using a modem (I'd never seen one before). Once connected, we ran the actual simulation the astronauts used when training for the first lunar landing. On my landing attempts, I blew several new craters in the moon, some hundreds of miles deep. Failing wasn't a problem (in fact it was hysterical). Doing it was radical; space-time boundaries were rewritten. Computers were virtual, interactive and seemingly unlimited. When I watched the lunar landing on television, I felt that I had been there; in some sense, I had been.

For a child of the Space Age, the computer was changing what was meant by the word "communication" itself. Communication was no longer just a matter of clarifying some inherent or objective truth. Communication was now a phenomenon that establishes what might be considered "truth" in the first place. Historically speaking, the dominant mode of social mediation establishes the realms of the possible and plausible (McLuhan). Morality, for example, made possible social organization, hunting, agriculture and myth—the stories we live by. Literacy made possible standardization and gave rise to humanism, conceptual thought and the scientific method.

Electronic, computer-mediated communication, is considered the third great revolution of evolution. Alvin Toffler called this the "third wave." Ernst Mandel called it "third stage." For Fredrick Jameson, it's "late-capitalism." And, for Jean-Francois Lyotard, "post-modernism." Others have called these times the post-industrial age of information—the age of communication. Across diverse literatures, the prophetic voice is the same. We are living in times of radical and rapid change. It is essential that we adapt so that we can excel in this environment. The study of communication prepares us to be highly skilled, *creative*, and employable in this electronic marketplace. However, it also prepares us to be highly educated, *perceptive*, and wise.

Hard Skills and Soft Skills

Just like computer hardware and software, the creative and the perceptive may be equated to hard skills (i.e., producing) and soft skills (i.e., critical thinking). Employers need both, and the study of communication considers both as a matter of course. Critical thinking is vital for practical reasons especially when seeking employment in a changing and unstable market. In fact, intellectual and creative skills are not necessarily opposites; we do not need to posit a false or unnecessary dichotomy.

Take filmmaking, for example. The production skills of scriptwriting, storyboarding, lighting, shooting and editing are enhanced when the filmmaker recognizes the critical skills and the power they have to change society. If we apply a critical lens to gendered film representations, for example, we must come to terms with the genealogy and structure of heteronormativity and whiteness. By seeking out images that radically challenge these conventions, we significantly raise the power of filmmaking. When creating and casting characters, we investigate a variety of sex/gender identities in classic and contemporary work, surveying literature that interprets and theorizes on the confluence of identity, body, sexuality, gender, class and race.

Computer-mediated communication, in the key of critical thinking, fosters understanding through personal empowerment and achievement using technological skills, intellectual challenges, and cultural insights to contribute to culture, community and self. Communication students are prepared for employment in all kinds of media and at all levels of mediation because disciplinary learning and hands on technical training are mutually supported. Indeed, the integration of theory and practice in computer-mediated communication appears as almost necessary because the same tool that we use to create, the computer, is the tool we use to research.

The computer is the virtual tool, shaped by its user. As I write, I'm running a web browser, email and note taking software. I have a mind-mapping program running on a second monitor so I can track the order of paragraphs, and plan tomorrow's class. When I finish writing, I'll open filmmaking and special effects software to complete a short film for which the soundtrack was already created using music production and mixing software. Computer-mediated communication provides us with the means to build our lives, and shape the lives of others, in the exciting worlds of radio, television, cinema, games, advertising, public relations and so on. Currently, the abilities of interactive computer-mediated communication are just being integrated into the market. Facebook, Twitter, and YouTube are just the beginning.

Why Storytelling is an Important Skill?

At first glance, the CMC field might appear excessively varied or unrelated, because what holds them together is not the technology itself; the technology is a tool, an intermediary. An archetype for intermediation is Hermes, the Greek god who interpreted the languages of the divine and the human. The formal study of interpretation is named Hermeneutics, after him. While there are many forms of hermeneutics, from the study of the Bible to the scientific method, one branch of study, philosophical hermeneutics, notes that interpretation is not only what we do; it's what we are. We are the interpreting animal. Interpretations, making sense of sensation and the senseless, must be put into expression if we seek to share our ideas with others. One method of communicating across the possibilities of computer-mediated communication, is storytelling.

Everyday life is saturated with stories. We talk to our family, friends and fellows by telling them the stories of our lives. Even the earliest records we have of mediated communication reveal narrative components. From the caves in Lascaux, to the tombs in Egypt, we see indications of temporal enactment or, put simply, stories. Birth. Life. Love. Conflict. Death. The most important lessons learned are passed down generation to generation as stories. As children, we learn about social norms and how we fit into society. Bed-time fairy tales. Vintage Muppet skits on YouTube. Disney movies.

Growing up, I watched "after school specials" that endeavored to teach my peers and me lessons in ethics and morality. We continue to be socialized with stories as we progress through school. Our textbooks give a sense of where we came from, and what we can aspire to. Journalists give insight, not only into our local communities, but also into cultures vastly different from our own. Music videos set expectations of gender roles telling and retelling tales of boy meets girl. Advertisers employ the power of storytelling for economic gain. We learn how we can run and win the race with Nike, or how we can provide for future generations with the right investment plans. However, we must be cautious. These stories are not always in our best interests.

Advertisements suggest beauty is something you buy. Music videos suggest that you never look good enough. Magazines suggest that you always have to be in new fashion. We encounter images that prey upon our weaknesses for the economic gain of others. We study communication through theories as diverse as psychoanalysis, deconstruction and feminism, as well as more traditional character, genre and narrative analysis, so we can learn how to see the functional and dysfunctional aspects of these stories. Being human means being a storyteller. Being a communication student means never taking a story for granted.

Stories that are pervasive, and those have been retold countless times, owe their longevity to the insight and instruction they provide us (here I am drawing on the collective work structuralism). <u>Cinderella</u>, for example, appears often as a mythological motif,' a 'mytheme.' The characters may change appearance (we see Anglo-European and African-American Cinderellas). Yet, the story still teaches us that it is normal to have mixed emotions about our parents. In the story, characters, for example, may be two sides of a coin. A character is not a person; a person is real while a character serves a narrative function. Fairy godmother: good. Evil stepmother: bad.

However, when we look at the names, the words, associating character with emotion, it's important to see critically that in this day and age the image of the "evil stepmother" is dysfunctional today, and multiple marriages is the norm. If the real stepmother is someone to value, then we can and *should* compose a new version of Cinderella. As professional communicators, we can work with the past to inform the present. Cinderella stories, such as Pretty Woman, with new characters that make sense in today's context are more relevant. The analysis of stories, genres, and characters provides communication students with a practical and historically relevant means of education for future activity.

Why the Study of Communication is Important?

The study of communication is important because, while we learn the skills of exciting careers, we also learn how to become informed citizens. We learn to see the story as a form of communication that is open to critique. Communication students shed their naiveté in favor of intelligence in order to recognize that the power that drives some stories is not in our best interest.

Delivery systems change, but the most common way we share experience is story. Stories are the neural network of communication studies. The communication students in schools, such as the one we've built at Shepherd University, examine the meaning of the stories they see around them, be they delivered in independent films or through the media.

Questions like, "How do these stories reflect and shape our culture?" We, the professional communicators, have the ability to bring about change.
Additionally, students develop their own personal visions and use them create new stories. They begin to understand that the thread of storytelling runs through all aspects of our lives. The Public Relations professional may call their story "spin." The political analyst will label storytelling "framing." The advertiser calls it "the pitch." The entrepreneur has an "elevator speech." A job seeker creates the resume. All are derivatives of storytelling.

Communication studies are dynamic, always open to new forms of expression. Graphic novel courses have become natural companions to the traditional communication curriculum. Understanding Comics by Scott McLoud, outlines the semiotics of comics. Semiotics is the study of the ways that a thing, like a color, or character or entire advertisement, points beyond itself, to conceptions (ideas, meaningless and values) such the "evil" stepmother or feminine beauty, for examples.

These ideas—feminine beauty--reside in larger mythological and ideological structures (romantic love, masculine power, capitalism). In the graphic novel, for example, we have the page, the pictures and the words (the tangible and physical); these are all material things that spark imagination and ideas (the intangible, ideal and spiritual). Studying the angles of view within a frame of a comic helps us visualize ideas for film. A temporal graphic allows us to study what will later be put into motion, temporality, in video. It is not accidental that many comics are now made into movies. Much of the heavy lifting has already been done. They are, for practical purposes, already storyboards.

It is important to hone our storytelling skills as best we can. As game culture becomes more and more prevalent, we can study game design to explore new ways to tell stories. While older games often relied on established plots, new games are different in that they are more open-ended, requiring a player's participation to make plot and character develop.

Games don't need to provide only pure entertainment (Wilson & Wright). The majority of corporations now use games to train employees. In many cases, the person responsible for the game design is somebody with a communication studies background who translates corporate objectives into a story that will teach and motivate players. Additional game design skills that will help communication professionals include teamwork and the ability to clearly communicate rules. Communication students must explore all aspects of storytelling in order to present their own messages most effectively. Because technological and intellectual abilities are both required, computer-mediated communication students who blend the hard-skills of production with the soft-skills of interpersonal understanding have an upper-hand on the market.

You must have Social Media Skills

Today, it seems everyone is on social media—from brands, to nonprofits, to politicians and celebrities, to the media and government agencies. As people turn to social media and the web to learn about everything from news events to new products, it has become vital that organizations meet this information demand. The potential benefits to organizations of creating and publishing content online are many. Traditionally, if an organization wanted to communicate directly with their public, they needed to either buy advertising or seek to get coverage by the media, such as newspapers and magazines. But with the proliferation of online publishing and the interactive capacities of blogs,

Twitter, Instagram, and more, these gatekeepers no longer stand in the way. Organizations can communicate directly with their audience in real time via text or multimedia. That means that in today's mediated world of smart phones and seemingly ubiquitous Internet access, all types of organizations need to, in a sense, become media producers.

And many have. Think of Red Bull. Red Bull is much more than an energy drink company. In October, 2012, the "Red Bull Stratos" project (put in quotation marks to connote the depth of branding) took place in which Felix Baumgartner, an Australian Skydiver jumped from the edge of space. And how did they promote this event and enable the public to take part? With an integrated social media campaign that saw record-breaking success. While possibly the most famous extreme sports event in recent memory, sponsored by Red Bull, it is but one example of how Red Bull entertains us. Check out Red Bull TV (http://www.redbull.tv/Redbulltv), where you can watch programming on extreme sports from motorsports to snowboarding.

At the same time, when we turn our eyes back to the event and its promotion, we see how a brand of soft drink is associated with entertainment and pleasure. The name Red Bull appears in this one paragraph seven times. The image of the product is infused with the energy of the "extreme" sports associated. When a thing and an idea become image, we are starring straight into the face of power.

As an educator, I find this relatively recent change in our media landscape fascinating. Companies need strategically minded, quick thinking, media savvy personnel to plan, produce, and publish their content to a growing list of social media platforms. Social media skills have become a must-have for students entering today's marketplace across a number of career options. No matter what field you want to work in related to the media, you need digital savvy.

The media world has changed dramatically. And it is essential that we adapt so that we can excel in this environment. Many young people today use social media in their personal lives, and they may feel that this experience means they are ready to use social media in the workplace. But using social media for your personal life and for your work are very different. In our Communication department, we seek to teach students to think about social media as tools for building and maintaining relationships with key audiences. Students are encouraged to think strategically.

They need to ask critical questions: To whom are they communicating? What are their audiences' needs? What are the ultimate goals of these relationships? What are the strengths and weaknesses? The critical thinking and production skills here get married to the ability to pervade the social space of the world wide web, because the web is no longer about "pages," but is about a media experience, a presence, that must appear on desktop, laptop, tablet and phone (Shockley-Zalabak).

In fact, social media has become a major component of the strategic communication field. According to the University of Southern California Strategic Public Relations Center's Generally Accepted Practices (GAP) study, from 2009 to 2011, public relations practitioners and agencies have become increasingly responsible for creating social media content for clients and managing their social media (Generally Accepted Practices VII Report, 2012). Our Strategic Communication program, where PR goes viral, empowers students to use social media, digital tools, and other forms of communication to produce purposeful, effective communication knowing that we, the creators and critical thinkers, are creating the very world in which we live.

Think about your Identity on the Internet

As you go out into the world, think about your identity on the Internet. How do you present yourself? What sort of things do you post on Twitter, on Vine? And how do those things make you look to the people that see them? Everything we communicate says something—whether it is what we intend to say or not. That is true for organizations as well as for people. Take 10 minutes and look through your recent social media postings. What would someone who never met you think about you based on what you post? To someone who has never met you in person, what you post online *is* your identity. We are now extended beyond ourselves; we appear to people unknown to us all over the world. To them, we are images, as they are to us. We know that organizations use public relations to deal with the issues of how and what they communicate.

Today, we have to think of ourselves in the same way. We advertise ourselves openly in every post. Employers thus have a first impression of you long before you get the chance to interview. Or, do you get the chance to interview after they examine your web presence? We still have the ability to make first impressions, but are we doing so responsible and knowingly? Are we doing so digitally? Your digital presence forms an image in the minds of your "audience," and that audience includes potential employers. It's no longer just clothing companies, sports teams, and rock bands making images, it's you too.

We compose with our fingers the entire digital universe. Computer-mediated communication is a set of employable production skills. It is also a way of thinking critically about the stories we live by. It is also the knowledge that we are *it*. We hold the power. Change the story and you change the society; it's not that easy, but it is fun. CMC is a marriage of expression and perception. We take ideas, sometimes vague and ethereal, and cast them in digital design. Words, pictures, sounds and video are the means to meld imagery and narrative, to shape ideas and inform audiences.

With the interactivity of the Web 2.0 technologies of Facebook, Twitter and so on, we, and our corporate partners, create the world dialogically. The strategy of design meets the tactics of interaction. We get to do it all. Each one of us makes a difference. Space-Age computing, relegated to the professional, has turned fully around to that Social-Age computing is in the hands of professional and amateur alike.

Chapter 3: The Need for Communicative Wisdom in an Age of Workplace Democracy. Professor Brent Yergensen, PhD

Dr Brent Yergensen, Ph.D. (University of Nebraska—Lincoln, 2011) is Assistant Professor and Chair of the Department of Communication at Dixie State University. As chair, he has created and administered numerous curricular and assessment programs for students in Communication Studies, Media Studies, and Film Production. As a scholar, he uses classical and contemporary rhetorical and critical theories to understand the underlying motives and assumptions of mediated messages. A specialist in the rhetoric of science who has presented numerous essays at competitive national and regional research conferences, his work has focused on the Enlightenment, string theory, and public scientific argument. In 2011 he received the Top Paper Award in the Rhetoric of Science and Technology Division at the National Communication Association. He has also published articles and book chapters on the rhetoric of popular culture, focusing on religious motifs and ideologies in popular film. A passionate teacher with a love for lively interactions with students, he has been a finalist for Teacher of the Year at Dixie State, and received the University of Nebraska's Recognition for Contributions to Students Award. He regularly teaches Rhetorical Theory and Criticism, Research Methods, Intercultural Communication, Argumentation and Critical Thinking, and Media & Society. His speaking style has led to invited seminars in public discourse, popular culture, and conflict management. He has served as a mediator of campus elections and policy discussions. His favorite part of life is spending time with his wife and children. He regularly volunteers as a youth sports coach, enjoys traveling, and zealously cheers for his Nebraska Cornhuskers during football season.

Introduction

As business models change as the result of technological breakthroughs, so too does the workplace environment. As a result, the expectations of employees loosen. People are given more freedoms, more leeway as technology allows people to publicly display the tastes, styles, and attitudes of their lifestyles. The need for what constitutes effective leadership in the workplace has also changed.

Ultimately, the contemporary workplace is a democratic setting. Leaders accept that workers want to share their ideas and offer feedback; and workers are aware that their input, participation, and ideas are welcome. We have arrived at an occupational state of respect not only for the highest executive's skill and managerial talents, but also for valuing the lowest worker's creativity and problem-solving skills. Students need communicative wisdom and training in the craft for succeeding in the new, open, and increasingly interactive workplace.

This shift toward democratic work environments comes as classical leadership models are dying in the wake of celebration for individuality in the workplace. Individuality has taken precedence. Workplace dynamics are shifting from the completion of assigned tasks as given to lower-level personnel, and are now being accomplished through group creativity[v]. The purpose of the Organization and Leadership emphasis at Dixie State University is utilization of a communicative approach that allows students to break down the traditional structure of power dynamics in the workplace through coursework in Organizational Communication and Communication and Contemporary Public Issues, as well as practical driven teamwork approaches with coursework in

Leadership & High Performance Teams. This approach is geared around new organizational paradigms where personnel are drawn to a workplace that is spearheaded by interactive leaders who encourage feedback from others.

Today's workplace demands that leaders be facilitators for generating ideas from those whom they supervise, just as much as they are distributors of tasks. The Communication degree at Dixie State University adopts a practically driven understanding of human behavior as the culprit but also the prescription for addressing workplace politics. Classes that engage in critical and cultural theory, such as Gender Communication and Intercultural Communication are meant to empower students with a complex and usable understanding of human diversity. Alteration in workplace culture requires greater competence in the craft of interaction in its increasingly rich and ever-more complicated situations where globalization's ramifications are certain[vi]. Such a democratic workplace setting can be honed with the application of communication theory.

As today's employees aren't mere task takers, but citizens of organizations, leaders must appreciate human complexity and have the interactive wisdom to navigate through and facilitate the flood of ideas that personnel have to offer. To prepare for the interactive workplace, students in the twenty-first century need training in interacting and operating in a globalized world that is ripe with personnel who have diverse backgrounds and beliefs. They must be empowered with the practical interaction skills and develop the savvy use of media-centered communicative tools for today's workplace democracy. Utilizing a holistic approach to interactive in its mediated and traditional settings, DSU Communication majors take coursework in new media production, media analysis, and journalistic ethics.

The Contemporary Workplace's Ache for Human Problem-Solving Skills

Today's workplace leaders will constantly face problems, and will need strategic interaction skills to address their personnel's challenges. Some problems are related to the organization's business ventures, yet others deal with internal errors and problems. Error emerges when political walls are put up by organizational personnel. Workplace politics is dangerous as it compartmentalizes ideas, stops sharp minds from interacting with one another, and hinders the infrastructure and the output of an organization's potential. As a result, organizations spend money to fix human errors.

Problem-solving is the immeasurable skill for today's employee. Employers crave to find new hires who have this gift[vii]. Because humans both create and solve problems, the Communication degree is focused on identifying, diagnosing, and providing executable prescriptions for exigencies in workplace, personal, and public settings. As a central component of Dixie State's Communication department's objectives, students take coursework in Argumentation and Critical Thinking, Persuasion, and in developing presentation skills with the use of technology in order to be ready for selling and collaboration between corporations with precision and complexity.

Strategic Communication as Antidote to Human-created Problems

Workplace problems can be financial due to clientele issues, technical due to equipment concerns, yet are very often human. This third type can be an expensive liability. People cost organizations dollars with unwarranted behaviors, personal challenges that play out in the work setting, unnecessary demands, and gossip. These behaviors distract, slow, and interfere with the purpose of the workplace. The democratic work setting magnifies this personal presence in the professional setting. The ability to fix these problems lies in the leader's capacity for strategizing on how to work with these individuals; and it takes wisdom to be able address such problems with care and strategy. The Communication curriculum is hot on the trail at addressing these contemporary behaviors and beliefs with theoretical explanations and skillful applications.

There is a demand for prudence to be used in helping personnel to properly focus and function on a daily basis. Students must be trained in the philosophy and practice of methodical interaction. Coursework in Interviewing allows DSU students to be able to collect information in professional settings as well as distinguish potential from others.

Further, as people communication more nonverbally than they do verbally, our Nonverbal Communication course offers students a theoretical toolset for understanding the tendencies and signs that are grounded in nonverbal decision. This talent requires a craft for grasping the complexity of human behavior and for skillfully addressing it. As an example outcome for methodical prudence, trained leaders will see others' ideas as culminations of their lived experiences. For employees, what is real in their minds emerges out of the experiences that make sense to them due to their unique backgrounds. Simply knowing this process by which humans assume what is real should effect and drive the leader's approach to working with their colleagues.

The communicatively-savvy leader therefore won't dismiss the ideas of others, even if he or she does not understand the thought process of the coworker. Rather, the leader will ask questions and thirst for more information on how the unique and perhaps even strange ideas seem executable to the person sharing their input. This skill is a recognition of the humanity of the individual, of lived experiences as genuine to the eye of the employee. Yet it also comes with a perseverance to hear and extract the employee's ideas, and therefore to find ways to connect that person's history and their idea into executable plans that work for the benefit of the organization. Certainly, such a process takes time, delicacy, and insight into how humans think and interact. The curriculum for navigating through this complex and messy human experience is in Communication.

A Long Tradition of Communication as Problem Solving

The need for wisdom to fix human error is not new. The same weakness also haunted humanity's first democracy, ancient Athens. Prudence was central to the upbringing of the politician or industry entrepreneur, who was trained to be communicatively intelligent. Aristotle[viii] referred to this type of practical wisdom as the "intellectual virtues." He describes how the capacity to be visionary, to deliberate, and to aim for the good of the collective's efforts are founded in effective analysis of situations and the use of persuasion in prescribing solutions. If "prudence is concerned with human goods," as he said, then the capacity to use interaction to solve problems is central to understanding and leading people who have complex personal histories and diverse attitudes (p. 134).

Aristotle links the search for what is best as being a deliberative process, and one that must be used by the trained leader who embodies the wisdom and capacity for building successful workplace interactions, "And the man who is good at deliberation generally is the one who can aim, by the help of his calculation, at the best of the good attainable by man" (p. 154). Training in the interactive craft was one of the original academic disciplines, and was used to train would-be politicians and industry workers for centuries. The need for it would return centuries later as today's student must be trained to operate effectively in the democratic workplace.

Scientization of Humanity, and the Industrialized Workplace

Despite centuries of being the focus of intellectual training, Aristotle's emphasis on practical and communicative ethics would fade out over time in the wake of positivistic science as the center for explaining the human condition. This changed humanity from being studied as the wise and interactive utilizer of mechanisms to becoming *the* systematic mechanism of study. Human thought and action were simplified. As a result, the Aristotelian virtue of deliberation and practical wisdom, while still alive over the ages, was relegated to sitting in the back row of scholarly inquiry and academic curriculum. The need for practical, human wisdom wouldn't return until democracy would again take center stage in the twenty-first century workplace.

Workplace Democracy and the Need for Communicative Wisdom

As humans, we have returned to a time of recognition of the complexity of human behavior. The twenty-first century is a time when social movements and policy have given place for voice to what could historically be called the laborer, the blue collar worker, or more sadly the 'muscle but not the brain.' Unions and the movement toward tolerance and zeal for diversity have created the open workplace environment. Workplace democracy, deliberation with employees, and the need for the return of prudence is stronger than ever because of the larger societal shifts of empowering marginalized groups. Students need curriculum that teaches them how to appreciate and work with human diversity with sensitivity, empathy, and appreciation for the complexity of conflicting ideas that will emerge out of coworkers' different backgrounds as well as their competing belief systems.

Further, the emergence of theories that are based on the critique of power has re-humanized the academic world. The study of humans as systems and structures is shifting to the study of abuse of power, its ramifications on its victims. Even further, the presence of mass media, groups' opportunities for resistance, and criticism of power structures has created a twenty-first century culture of diverse opinions, organized resistance, and the continual push for equality. In regards to the professional world, the result is a need to hire organizational personnel who are fully aware of the ramifications of the communicative choices they make. They will use power to obtain ideas from and not to suppress others. They will be aware of how their subtle decisions, good or bad, can have far-reaching ramifications on their status with supervisors, peers, and even subordinates.

Training in theories and models designed for practical wisdom empowers students with a careful sense of caution that is both self-reflective and poignantly built on creating and sustaining healthy workplace relationships. For without healthy workplace relationships, politics reigns, distrust emerges, and people come to disdain one another. The maintenance for addressing these challenges requires the leader who can find and illuminate the "human goods" that Aristotle says is achievable. Such is the purpose of the Communication degree.

To be prepared to take on such a performance, the Communication degree trains students in the following skills, which are based on the development of workplace competencies: 1. Teamwork in the corporate world that demands collaboration to accomplish organizations' goals, 2. Management styles designed to function in a time of the marriage of personnel's professional and personal lives, and 3. Presentation skills that lend credence to an organization's image, livelihood, and reputation.

Teamwork in an Increasing Collaborate Workplace

One of the virtues of workplace democracy is the demand for transparency from both companies and their workers. In the age of the empowered individual, people have married their personal and professional lives. One cannot fully separate his or her professional persona from their personal identity. Privacy isn't an option in a time of social media. Further, few organizations monitor personal styles with grooming and dress codes anymore. As an extension of personal transparency, accountability for one's workplace tasks must be explained, perhaps even to an audience amidst the age of human resources. In many companies, human resource departments monitor and probe the daily work environment. Employers keep their employees in check.

To share accountability and to pursue enriched success, the teamwork format for doing business is reigning. In-house workplace monitoring demands it. Peers keep each other on task. Social media creates a sense of individuality. Human resources puts the rule book in the face of all personnel. Today's employee is his or her own empowered ethical theorist in the wake of proud individuality. We want to express our individuality, and do not shy away from having it monitored. This new employee lifestyle must be lead in a way that their talents are discovered and utilized and that they are treated with strategic delicacy, all based on the leader's ability for the interactive craft.

The Communication degree walks students through the process of team development, explores how to avoid and if needs be manage damaging personalities from domineering the workplace, teaches how to ensure and combine minds to maximize utilization, and offers the theoretical explanations of, benefits of, and application of synergistic teamwork interaction. These analytic skills can help an organization's economic goals, as well as temper internal politics. Students who leave college with a Communication degree possess a complex understanding and strategic framework of how to succeed in group settings. For the student who becomes a new hire, manager, or executive, this skill alone can make or break a career.

Management Styles for the Cohabitation of Professional and Personal Lives

If workplace democracy forces us to be personalities as well as representatives of organizations, the emergent leader is one who adopts a meek approach to the personnel whom he or she guides. While meekness is often seen as a passive trait, such passivity is, in the workplace that celebrates democracy, accompanied with a wise, methodical, and calculating reservation on the part of the leader. Reservation is more often than not warranted in situations where tempers, egos, and ignorance can drive people off task. The communicative leader's patient wisdom is the outcome of holistic and deep understandings of human interaction. Lack of judgment allows personnel to confidently share their ideas with colleagues and leaders. Personnel will always represent their political, ideological, and even religious views in the workplace, even if doing so subtly. The democratic workplace warrants their right to do so, being that people do not need to hide who they are in fear of reprisal for their beliefs and lifestyles in the twenty-first century of tolerance and policy-driven diversity.

Therefore, the foolish leader would manage in a way that dismisses their co-workers' individuality. Students must be shown how to carefully communicate in a way that they are ever-aware of where the corporate world has arrived, especially in corporate settings.

The Communication degree introduces students to frameworks on how to discover and address the histories and motives of lifestyles, and the value that comes from utilizing diverse perspectives and histories. To each individual, his or her perspectives make perfect sense. The challenge is in helping people to share that the organization can extract all the data it needs to find its best course of action. This will enrich the leader's resources because the Communication curriculum includes theoretical explanations of how people are constantly doing face work. If a leader is aware as to why his or her employees are constantly working to manage their images, then prudence, in its comprehensive explanations, empowers the leader to be able to address individual people who have individual interests.

To utilize such a meek understanding of those they lead, students in Communication obtain training in the complexity of human development of beliefs and attitudes. The purpose of the Communication discipline is to diagnose problems and prescribe solutions for the most complicated and complex element of the workplace, its people and their behaviors. Perhaps the most challenging course students take is Small Group Communication because of the context in which students are required to develop relationships, brainstorm about exigencies to study, and then as a group function as a team that can practically address challenges. Such is a challenging concept for students as it stretched expectations beyond the traditional classroom expectations of writing the term paper. Yet in the end, students have been introduced to observing and operating in authentic settings where workplace politics and personalities are at work.

Presentation Skills as Central to Organizations' Makeup and Success

The most prominent result of any democracy is the priceless gift of free speech. How an organization is presented can lead to its profitable success, or its disastrous fall by having a tarnished reputation. Further, organizations are represented by its people; its administrators in the public eye, its representatives in public relations and advertising, and in conversation between its personnel with the daily public.

In order to survive companies rely on collaboration with other organizations, as well as the accumulation of new clientele. The success of these two endeavors is done by savvy organizational advocates who are aware of the delicacy of word choices when it comes to closing deals. These advocates know they are persuading other human beings who represent either themselves or entire organizations as clients, and that success is accomplished almost entirely on an interactive level in the late stages of negotiation.

The art of persuasion is therefore an immeasurable craft for students to master. While charisma and personality cannot be taught, meticulous observation of the behaviors and feedback of one's audience can indeed be developed with training. There is a practical philosophy to reading others' behaviors and strategically addressing audiences in the Communication degree.

As a resource for business-related presentations, the necessity of public speaking is as important in today's business setting as it is to the politician and the religious leader. Organizations live and die by how their personnel play for them in the game of deal-making, image-creating, and relationship building. At the introductory level, DSU's Communication majors take courses in Public Speaking and Interpersonal Communication to engender toolsets for competency in public and small setting.

Students in Communication program practice presenting in order to be aware of an audience's immediate feedback in a presentation, how to adjust to an audience's needs, and how to develop an individual presentation style that ensures sincerity, clarity, and poise with audiences. If communication skills can make or break deals, than the philosophy of communication is the curriculum for successful business.

Conclusion

At Aristotle's time, the study of communication was central to industry and citizenship. One succeeded because of his or her communicative gifts in law, entertainment, and military. In the current age of democracy, students face the same challenge: success is driven and measured by the interactive craft. The rules have changed since ancient Athens. Business models center around the use of technology. How wise is the man or woman who enters the workplace knowing how to utilize technology to build trust, to reach out persuasively, to see value in the perspectives of others, and to use prudence in a way that is careful, relationship-based, and as a result opens the door to earning the trust and respect of coworkers and clients. Communicative wisdom creates and promises the longevity of a career.

Chapter 4: The Communication Major – Professor Thomas Hugh Feeley, Ph.D

Dr Thomas Hugh Feeley (Ph.D., University at Buffalo, the State University of New York) is Professor and Chair of Communication at University at Buffalo, the State University of New York. He also holds faculty appointments in Family Medicine and Nursing. His research program centers on the design, implementation, and evaluation of health campaigns in the area of solid organ donation. His research has been funded since 2003 by the Health Resources Services Administration (HRSA/NIH) social and behavioral grants program. His scholarship also examines social influence processes (e.g., social networks, persuasion) in organizational and health settings. In addition to various book chapters and white papers, Feeley has authored over 75 refereed journal articles and his work has appeared in Human Communication Research, Communication Monographs, Journal of Communication and several other top-tier journals in the fields of communication, public health and social psychology.

Common Elements to the Major in Communication

The Communication Major is a commonly misunderstood program of study despite its popularity as an undergraduate major. This misunderstanding is further complicated by the various titles given to the major which range from "Journalism & Mass Communication," to "Speech & Rhetoric." Regardless of the title and the specific content of the curricula, there are common elements to the major in communication in my experience. My perspective on the major is from two experiences in the communication major.

My primary experience is being an undergraduate (BA, 1991) and graduate student (PhD, 1996) in the major at University at Buffalo, The State University of New York where I am currently Professor and Department Chair (UBCOM hereafter). UBCOM's undergraduate program offers a B.A. in the major and courses are a mix of theoretical and applied offerings. Many of the latter courses (e.g., public speaking, promotional writing) are taught by professionals in the field of public communication whereas the theory courses are traditionally taught by tenure-track and full-time adjunct faculty.

My second experience stems from 5+ years on the

faculty at Geneseo College (State University of New York) who also offers a B.A. program in communication and my 14 years on the faculty at UBCOM who offers BA, MA, and PhD degrees in Communication. The Geneseo and UBCOM programs are similar in their mix of theoretical and applied courses. Applied courses instruct students about communication *skills* (speaking, writing) and about *forms* of public communication (public relations, advertising).

Choosing the Undergraduate COM Major

Students should choose the COM major if they are interested in *studying* the forms and potential influences in communication. I stress *interested* in studying (and thereby better understanding) communication processes (e.g., use of Facebook, relationships, media effects) and not necessarily choosing COM as means to starting a career, as too often students overlook their course of study and focus on their future career prospects.

Choosing COM for entirely career-driven reasons is a mistake. To properly understand the field and communication processes, a student must dedicate herself to *studying* the history and theories of communication. The core of the field has always been and I suspect will always be in the strategic, intentional or purposeful use of communication messages and their delivery to shape or reinforce attitudes and behaviors toward senders' goals.

Also core is learning the effects or ramifications of the use of certain messages. Thus, students ought to learn the social psychology of communication processes and also learn the skills to appropriately and effectively send and exchange messages to/with a given constituency. The major remains a large one across campuses due to its wide appeal to different students as well to its wide appeal to employers who seek job candidates who possess the skills and knowledge base covered the COM major.

Pursuing Graduate Work in COM

A student should pursue a graduate degree in communication if s/he is interested in either becoming a professor of communication or if s/he wishes to learn more about specific communication theories or processes through a dedicated research program. Most graduate programs, especially at the doctoral level, have tuition scholarships that carry modest stipends with them to subsidize a student's education.

In turn the student is often asked to serve as a teaching assistant or perform some other administrative function (e.g., website maintenance, advisement). Scholarships are available for both domestic and international students and the field is becoming increasingly more international. Research programs are typically divided between theoretical and research-intensive programs and applied programs. A handful of programs include production-related courses in the graduate curriculum, such as Indiana University of Pennsylvania. Applied programs usually offer the M.A. degree only in COM or have some other title more specific to the curricula (e.g., Public Relations, Advertising) that is relevant to the course of COM study. My own research is in the area of persuasion and social influence – I am interested in what message strategies are more influential in achieving one's communication goals.

An important consideration when considering graduate work in COM is considering the amount of overlap between one's undergraduate degree and the graduate degree in terms of course and internship content. If the graduate degree's coursework is largely redundant with an undergraduate degree's curriculum, one might consider an alternative graduate program or an internship. An attractive pair of degrees would have one earn an applied MA in COM with a degree in business or in the humanities. A graduate degree would provide a solid theoretical and research methods base for graduates to use in their career pursuits in the public communication sector.

A doctoral degree in COM is warranted if one wishes to pursue a career in academia or research. In terms of becoming a professor in a communication department, there are two types of tenure-track appointments in the United States. The most common type of appointment is becoming a professor at college and teaching a 3 to 4 course load (per semester) to undergraduates. Stated differently, the professor's main charge is instruction and advisement of undergraduate students. The second type of appointment is less common and requires faculty to teach fewer sections (typically 2 per term) and requires faculty members to conduct original research, write and conduct grants, and advise graduate theses and dissertations. There are certainly forms of appointments that fall somewhat in between the instructional and research-intensive extremes. For example, some positions have 3 courses per term with 1 course in the MA program and modest research expectations.

Advice

Here is my advice from 18+ years as a professor, scholar and chair in the field of communication. Take a proactive role in your education and take it personally. Earn high marks, get involved and undertake various internships and make them count. Too often students complain they didn't "get enough" from an internship while they passively react to instructions from supervisors, who are often quite busy. Don't be reactive, be proactive and take initiative. The COM degree can matter little to some and matter a ton to many but it is student dependent. Use theory and research to understand audiences and to measure success and document your experiences in detail for future employers and opportunities. There are great careers for COM majors and I have dozens of students working on Madison Avenue in New York, in Washington D.C., and all over the world. These students capitalized on their coursework and applied experiences and took initiative.

My second form of advice is to always ask, "Why?" Why does a certain article get front page? Why do certain commercials capture our attention versus other commercials? What posts in Facebook get more comments compared to other posts? Answers to questions regarding the nature of human communication are the domain of communication theories. It is certainly important to identify critical important relationship but just as more important to understand why certain relationships exist. This is how we push knowledge forward in the field of communication.

Chapter 5: Why Study Communication? – Professor Dawn O. Braithwaite, PhD

Dr. Dawn O. Braithwaite, is a Willa Cather Professor and Department Chair at the University of Nebraska-Lincoln. She studies how people in personal and family relationships interact and negotiate family change and challenges. She studies discourse dependent and understudied families, communication rituals, and dialectics of relating in stepfamilies and among voluntary (fictive) kin. Dr. Braithwaite has authored over 100 articles and is co-editor or co-author of five books including Family Communication: Cohesion and Change (9th edition) and Engaging Theories in Interpersonal Communication (see http://un-lincoln.academia.edu/DawnBraithwaite). She received the National Communication Association's Brommel Award for Outstanding Contributions in Family Communication, the division's Book Award, the University of Nebraska-Lincoln College of Arts & Sciences Award for Outstanding Research in Social Science. She was named the Western States Communication Association Distinguished Scholar for 2014. She is currently a Senior Fellow with the Council on Contemporary Families. Dr.

Braithwaite is a Past President of the Western States Communication Association and received the association's Distinguished Service Award. She was President of the National Communication Association in 2010.

Why Study Communication?

We see the study of communication as central to personal, professional, and civic life. In our particular program we describe:

The mission of the Department of Communication Studies is to examine human symbolic activity as it shapes and is shaped by relationships, institutions, technologies, and cultures. This work concerns the creation, analysis, and critique of messages ranging from face-to-face to digital media contexts. The department's research and teaching devote particular attention to scholarly initiatives aimed at understanding and explaining the role of communication in (a) facilitating civic engagement mediating public controversies, and organizing for social change (b) constituting individual and family health, promoting healthy behaviors, and helping persons navigate relational challenges, and (c) creating, maintaining, and challenging personal, social, and community identity in a complex and diverse world.

In addition, "our research and teaching focus is on public advocacy, argument analysis, communicating across difference, negotiation and conflict management, family interaction, and relational competencies."

In the U.S., employers regularly list communication as the #1 skill or competency they are seeking. For our undergraduate students we focus on the core competencies of Advocate, Negotiate, and Relate. Our graduates have an excellent employment rate at a wide variety of careers in the public, private and not-for-profit sectors. The department has approximately 175 undergraduate majors and 35 graduate students, most of whom are pursuing the doctoral degree.

Communication Research at UNL

The Communication Studies Department is organized around three cross-cutting scholarly initiatives that guide our research and graduate teaching: Civic Engagement, Health and Well-being, and Identity and Difference. The department offers graduate emphases in Interpersonal, Family and Intergroup Communication and Rhetoric & Public Culture. We introduce undergraduates to these three areas by focusing on the ways in which communication helps them Advocate, Negotiate and Relate across contexts.

Civic Engagement focuses on the role of communication in facilitating public participation, mediating public controversies, and organizing for social change and citizen involvement.

Topics in this scholarly initiative include:
- Public deliberation about science and technology, moral controversies, and political issues
- Forms of organizing enabling and constraining participation and voice
- Historical analysis of how citizens mobilize for social change
- Stakeholders in community consensus-building
- Uses of new media to spark citizenship practices and engagement across social divides
- Family socialization of pro-social behavior and civic engagement

Health and Well-being focuses on the role of communication in understanding and explaining individual and relational health, promoting healthy behaviors, and helping persons navigate challenges.

Topics in this scholarly initiative include:
- Interacting and negotiating family change and challenges as it relates to health and well-being.
- Mental, physical, and relational health outcomes of individual and collaborative storytelling, accounting, and communicated perspective-taking
- Family communication and psychosocial well-being in nontraditional families (e.g., interfaith, multiethnic step-, lesbian and gay headed, voluntary)
- Communication challenges and designing interventions for health care teams, patients, and family caregivers in the context of serious or terminal illness

Identity and Difference focuses on the role of communication in constituting identity in a complex and diverse world.

Topics in this scholarly initiative include:
- Rhetorics of identity, power, and difference in public argument and address
- Marginalized groups exercising civic agency
- Family socialization and influence on worldviews, attitudes, and orientations toward others

- Role of communication in creating and enacting nontraditional families
- Discourses of racism and poverty in contemporary political discourse
- How various forms of organizing enable and constrain the development of voice

The university and the department welcomes international students. In recent years we have had graduate students join us from China, Ethiopia and Nigeria. While the department has no scholarship funding apart from Graduate Teaching Assistantships students should consult the Graduate Studies webpage for application and funding information: http://www.unl.edu/gradstudies/prospective/inter national

Translational Scholarship

Communication scholars engage in the creation of knowledge through basic research and have a strong commitment to translational scholarship that can make a difference in our diverse communities. Some scholars build this translational element into their research design, testing the usefulness or efficacy of communication intervention. Other scholars concentrate on bringing their research into communities via blogs, working with the media, and presentations to various audiences who would benefit from the research. For many scholars the skills of translating scholarship must be developed as this has not historically been a part of graduate school training.

Best Practices

Our departmental newsletter, the "COMMHusker" features interviews with undergraduate and graduate alumni. We ask them for their advice to current students and here is what they have said:

Talk to as many professionals, within your field(s) of interest, as possible. Ask questions. Start networking. Do this sooner than later.

I would advise any commutation student, undergrad or grad, to not place arbitrary limits on yourselves. You may not think you are a "theory person" or a "qualitative person", etc., but you will grow in unexpected ways by learning divergent perspectives... When you graduate you really are done with classes. Thus, learn to stretch your mind now!

For undergraduates, participate in an internship that provides professional experience in a field that you may want to pursue after graduation. For graduate students, cultivate your relationships with your peers and with the faculty so that you build a strong, supportive network of colleagues.

Use your summers wisely. My time at UNL certainly prepared me well for the work I do now, but I would not have even known about this position had I not spent two summers interning in Washington, DC. I encourage students to use the summers to explore the "real world" side of the profession they believe they are interested in pursuing. It will either confirm that interest or send them in another direction--both of which are extremely helpful to know before you take a job!

My advice would be for you to foster the relationships with the faculty and the other students who are currently there with you. These begin the relational networks that are so important in your life and career that will carry you forward in whatever you decide to do. Also, appreciate the opportunity to read important works and have big conversations because, even if you choose to become faculty in a supportive department, it will become more and more difficult to be able to do these bigger picture things... You can decide what kind of career you want and what kind of scholarly life you want to pursue, but it is important to lay the good groundwork while you are there.

Chapter 6: Communication is a Hot, Relevant, and Exciting Academic Discipline! – Professor Gary Kreps, PhD

Gary L. Kreps is a University Distinguished Professor of the Department of Communication at George Mason University. He teaches undergraduate and graduate courses in Communication Research, Health Communication, Organizational Communication, Consumer-Provider Health Communication, Health Communication Campaigns, and E-Health Communication. Dr. Kreps received his BA and his MA in Communication from the University of Colorado, Boulder and his PhD from the University of Southern California. Dr. Kreps' areas of expertise include health communication and promotion, information dissemination, organizational communication, information technology, multicultural relations, risk/crisis management, health informatics, and applied research methods. His published work includes more than 350 books, articles, and monographs concerning the applications of communication knowledge in society.

There are Ample Professional Opportunities for Communication Graduates

Communication is one of the most relevant and exciting academic disciplines! We study the integral process of communicating that enables us to elicit cooperation in solving problems and adapting to challenges. It is the ultimate survival mechanism for humanity. Mastery in communication will serve students well over their entire lives. This is a hot, relevant, and exciting academic discipline!

Recent evidence has shown that the communication discipline is growing rapidly, with increasing numbers of career opportunities for communication graduates. In fact, data suggest that the supply of Ph.D. graduates in communication may not adequately meet the demand for new faculty to teach in departments and schools of communication where undergraduate and graduate enrollments are burgeoning. Professional recruiters are interested in attracting communication graduates to job openings in a wide variety of fields.

There are a broad range of career opportunities available to communication graduates. Students who earn undergraduate degrees in communication studies can work in many different professional fields, including public relations, advertising, sales, administration, editing, education, training, and media production, marketing, and distribution. There are ample professional opportunities for communication graduates is business, retail, corporate, educational, health care, social service, and non-profit sectors. Surveys of corporate leaders have shown that the development of advanced communication competencies, such as effective speaking, writing, listening, media production, negotiation, conflict management, and relationship development skills are critically important for professional success.

Moreover, the development of advanced understanding of communication processes and competencies in effective communication will serve individuals well in all aspects of their personal and professional lives. Communication is the essential social process used to engender cooperation, collaboration, and problem solving in society. Students of communication who learn how to use communication strategically to accomplish their goals across different contexts and with different audiences will have a distinct advantage in developing successful personal and professional lives.

Earning a Research Degree in Communication

Earning a research degree in communication will enable students to learn how to rigorously evaluate the effectiveness of communication programs and processes in many different settings. They will learn how to conduct survey research to gather data from different audiences with questionnaires, interviews, and focus group discussions. They will learn how to conduct ethnographic examinations of communication contexts through direct and participant observations, as well as from data gathered from cultural informants. They will learn how to conduct experimental tests of the influences of independent variables on dependent variables to determine both relationships between and the effects of communication processes on relevant outcomes. They will also learn how to analyze communication texts, documents, performances, and productions with content, discourse, interaction, and rhetorical analyses. These research skills will enable communication graduates to evaluate communication situations and activities to design evidence-based strategies for achieving communication goals.

At George Mason University (GMU) we prepare our undergraduate and graduate students in all aspects of communication research, helping them to become effective consumers and producers of both quantitative and qualitative research methods. We want our students to be able to design research studies, using a range of communication methods and tools, to address specific communication issues effectively. We also take an applied focus to the study of communication, emphasizing the pragmatic applications of communication knowledge in modern life. We conduct research examining the best ways to use communication to promote health, preserve the environment, and enhance political decision making, locally, nationally, and globally. Information about admission and scholarships can be found at the GMU website (www.gmu.edu).

My Research Interests

My own research program examines how evidence-based and culturally-sensitive communication interventions, utilizing multiple strategic media, technologies, and messages, can reduce health inequities and promote global health. I use rigorous and revealing multi-methodological field data to guide strategic dissemination of relevant health information and support for consumers, caregivers, and providers to guide informed health decisions/actions across the continuum of care. I am a scientific advisor to many major federal agencies (such as the NIH, NCI, CDC, AHRQ, FDA, VHA, PCORI, SAMHSA, and NLM), foreign governments (including China, Japan, Singapore, Korea, Switzerland, Italy, Israel, Canada, Ireland, and Australia), research firms and health organizations. I collaborate with diverse community groups and organizations to help vulnerable populations, including people confronting serious socioeconomic challenges, individuals with low levels of health literacy, members of disenfranchised groups, immigrants, and people confronting serious, debilitating, and stigmatized health conditions. My work is designed to enhance informed health decision-making and build relevant support mechanisms through active community collaborations that refine health practices and improve health outcomes.

My research focuses on the information and support needs of consumers, providers, and caregivers confronting cancers, HIV/AIDS, heart disease, chronic health problems, mental health problems, and serious health risks/crises. I develop and evaluate strategic evidence-based communication interventions (educational programs, information technologies, communication policies, and practices) to promote informed decision making, early detection, health promoting behaviors, high quality and collaborative care, social support, successful survivorship, health advocacy, and well-being. I work locally (coordinating the Fairfax County Health Literacy Initiative community-based collaborative), nationally (introducing the Health Information National Trends Survey, HINTS), and internationally (introducing the HINTS-China research program and the Global Advocacy Leadership Academy, GALA, program).

My research, reported in more than 400 scientific publications, has been supported by major government agencies, foundations, and international organizations. My publications are heuristic, generating more than 7,000 citations so far (according to Google Scholar). Theories that I have developed examining communication and health outcomes, such as the Relational Health Communication Competence Model, have been validated, extended, and applied in many studies. My work in health informatics has helped introduce, refine, and institutionalize important new e-health programs and applications. My current research projects are introducing strategic new communication programs that promise to promote health and well-being for vulnerable and at-risk populations locally, nationally, and around the world.

Integrating Theory, Research, and Practice through Teaching

Communication research has the potential to help inform decision making about professional practices and policies across many sectors of society. However, communication researchers must address important research questions, gather revealing data, and report research results in ways that key public audiences can access, understand and use.

It is also important for communication scholars to make their work easily accessible, understandable, and relevant to different audiences. This means that communication scholars must engage in careful audience analysis to identify the topics and issues that are most relevant to key audiences, the best channels of communication to utilize to reach these audience members, and the most appropriate messages, terminology, and examples to help audience members fully understand the relevance of communication research for them.

It is important to engage in relevant, personal, and passionate communication education to help learners to not only develop important new academic knowledge, but to integrate what they learn into their personal and professional lives. I am committed to using pedagogy to influence both research and practice.

In my courses I critically examine cutting-edge research and help students become influential scholars, communicators, entrepreneurs, and advocates. I want students to use what they learn to achieve personal and professional goals, as well as to help others effectively confront challenging issues. Teaching is an essential part of my mission to raise consciousness about health promotion, address complex and challenging health communication issues, generate new ideas and strategies for solving health problems, and introduce new programs, projects, and activities to promote individual and public health. Through my teaching, I integrate theory, research, and practice.

COMMUNICATION FOR THE UNDECIDED STUDENTS, THEIR MAJOR &
CAREER ADVISORS, AND PARENTS: WHY STUDY COMMUNICATION?

Chapter 7: Why Study Communication? – Professor Kristina Horn Sheeler, PhD

Dr Kristina Horn is the Chair and Associate Professor at the Department of Communication Studies. She obtained her Ph.D. from Indiana University (Bloomington) in 2000. Dr Horn's academic interests include political communication, gender, and public identity, studying the ways in which political identity is rhetorically constructed and contested in popular media. She has authored/co-authored books including **Woman President: Confronting Postfeminist Political Culture** *and,* **Governing Codes: Gender, Metaphor, and Political Identity***.*

What is Communication?

Communication Studies as an academic discipline is devoted to the study of human message-use as a complex *process* through which meanings are co-constructed in a variety of contexts. We approach communication not simply as a tool, but as a *process* through which we create, change, and understand our world. In other words, communication *matters. Communication does*

Copyright © 2019 by the Curious Academic Publishing   Page 121 *things.*

Let me provide one brief example. On April 4, 1968, Senator Robert F. Kennedy was scheduled to give a campaign speech in Indianapolis, Indiana.[ix] He was running for US president. On the way to Indianapolis, Senator Kennedy learned that Martin Luther King, Jr. had been assassinated. Senator Kennedy's speech was scheduled in the middle of one of Indianapolis's African-American neighborhoods. Then-mayor Richard Lugar advised Kennedy against going into the neighborhood to make the speech; his safety could not be guaranteed. Kennedy went anyway.

When he arrived at 17th and Broadway, the crowd had been waiting for a long time and had no idea what had happened that day. They did not have immediate access to information on cell phones like we do today. Kennedy stepped onto the back of a flatbed truck to give his speech. Just before he began to speak, he asked, "Do they know?" The answer was "No." In that instant, the purpose of Kennedy's speech changed from a campaign speech to a eulogy, and the importance of his speech grew exponentially.

Senator Kennedy informed the crowd that Martin Luther King, Jr. had been killed; the crowd gasped.

His next words were critical for they could determine the action of the crowd later that night. Senator Kennedy reminded the crowd of King's life work and legacy. Urging those in the audience to remember King's dream, he compelled the crowd to "dedicate ourselves . . . to tame the savageness of man and to make gentle the life of this world." In just six short minutes Kennedy eulogized a great man and convinced the crowd to disperse peacefully. Indianapolis was the only major city in the US that did not erupt into violence that night, and many believe it was due, in part, to Kennedy's speech. Kennedy's words *did something* that night—they delivered bad news, compelled a crowd to recall King's legacy, and urged the crowd to go forth and live King's dream. His words created in that situation a reality that changed the lives of everyone in attendance that night and made an impact all over the country.

Certainly not all of us will find ourselves in a situation equal to the gravity of Senator Kennedy's purpose that night. However, that does not mean our communication transactions are any less compelling. Each of us has the opportunity to engage in the process of communication with a mindfulness that can shape and change our relationships, our workplaces, our neighborhoods, public politics, our personal health, and yes, even our nation or globe. Communication shapes the most foundational fabric of our lives; it *creates* the worlds in which we live. It is for these reasons, and many others, that communication study is such a rich, growing, and significant area of inquiry in our globalized economy.

What is Communication Study as an Academic Discipline?

The academic discipline of Communication Studies began as the study of rhetoric in Ancient Greece in roughly the 4th century BCE. Rhetoricians were teachers of speech who recognized a practical need to be filled. People needed communication instruction in order to learn the art of rhetoric, or persuasion—to defend themselves in courts of law, to acquire land, to win votes, to make laws, to praise the worthy or condemn the unfit—to create democratic communities. One of the first treatises on rhetoric, Aristotle's *The Rhetoric*, includes many of his observations and recommendations on the art of rhetoric, a manuscript that is influential in our understanding of rhetorical theory even today. In other words, communication study at its root is a theory-driven *and* practical, applied area of study, and it continues to be so today.

In the twenty-first century, the study of human communication has grown from its rhetorical roots to include a wide range of inquiry from social scientific, humanistic, and critical-cultural scholars. Areas of communication study may include, but are certainly not limited to: organizational, political, international and intercultural, interpersonal, legal, media, conflict resolution, group dynamics, public address, rhetorical, and even visual and health communication. To learn more about the study of communication, visit the National Communication Association's (NCA) web page, especially "What is Communication?" and related links.[x] This is the largest disciplinary association in the US devoted to the theoretical and practical study of human communication in its various contexts.

Career Opportunities for a Communication Major

From the brief list of areas of study above, it should be clear that future career opportunities are great. The knowledge and skills that one learns as a communication major include not simply disciplinary or theoretical knowledge, but strong writing, speaking, research, needs-assessment, problem-solving, and critical thinking skills. The strength of a communication major is that it prepares you for a variety of careers, not simply a specific career which may not be around one year from now.

Further, the flexibility of a communication studies major allows you to position yourself for careers that may not even exist yet. You are only limited by your interests and drive. For example, one recent communication studies graduate from my university saw a need in an organization and persuaded that organization to hire her to fill that need in a position that didn't exist. She was successful. In other words, the ability to diagnose and assess organizational needs and pose solutions to those needs is at the core of what you learn as a communication studies major. And it can position you in exciting career opportunities that you create yourself!

According to the *Princeton Review* in 2014, communication is among the top 10 college majors.[xi] And it's no wonder. According to *Forbes*, of the 10 skills that employers desire in their employees, the majority are skills and knowledge you will learn by studying communication.[xii] *Yahoo! Education* lists Communication as one of the top five "in-demand" degrees to start now[xiii] with the lowest levels of unemployment.[xiv] It was Warren Buffet who famously remarked: "If you improve your communication skills, I will guarantee you that you will earn fifty percent more money over your lifetime."[xv] Clearly majoring in communication, and taking the study of communication seriously, can prepare you for a lifetime of success. For more information on communication as a major and communication careers, check out the NCA publication *Pathways to Communication Careers in the 21st Century*.[xvi]

Why Begin a Research Degree in Communication Studies?

Communication research continues to address important issues and problems in our global world. In areas as diverse as political communication, democratic citizenship, interpersonal and relational communication, organizational communication, crisis management, community engagement, risk and health communication, intercultural communication and everything in between, communication scholars are asking important questions that have the ability to change people's lives, such as:

- How can we create a more engaged citizenry?
- How can we reframe the narratives in place in US political culture that impede the election of a woman president?
- How can racial humor create an opportunity for more productive conversations about race and racism?

- What communication strategies best help an organization manage and recover from a crisis?
- How can romantic partners recover from a lack of intimacy?
- What role does family communication play in navigating the loss of a loved one?
- What are the most effective strategies to use when communicating about marriage-equality in the state of Indiana?
- How can I create a more collaborative workplace culture?
- How can I convince more people to be involved in my neighborhood association?
- What are the best communication strategies and channels to use during a natural disaster such as a hurricane?
- How do couples manage private information about miscarriage?
- How and when do Latino children take on parental roles when assisting their parents in multi-lingual environments?
- What intercultural barriers must be overcome to convince people in Kenya to use mosquito nets?
- What narratives might be most receptive to rural Indiana citizens when it comes to the importance of regular mammograms?

Why should you take on a research degree in communication? To impact people's lives and make better worlds. That answer may sound overly idealistic, but it's true. Communication research really does make a difference in people's lives on a daily basis. As I wrote earlier, *communication matters. Communication does things.* More effective communication can impact positively relational and community problems, citizen participation, organizational crises and global concerns. Even personal health can be improved through more effective public communication. Those are some of the reasons to take on a research degree in communication.

Studying Communication at IUPUI

My own university, Indiana University-Purdue University Indianapolis (IUPUI) is developing a nationally recognized health communication program. In fact, we have the only PhD program in the US that focuses specifically on health communication. Students entering our undergraduate and graduate programs in health communication will have the opportunity to study health communication in a variety of theory-based and clinical contexts including interpersonal health, international and intercultural health, health in mediated-contexts, health campaigns, and privacy-issues in health contexts.

My university also offers a strong undergraduate degree in Communication Studies generally as well as a MA in Applied Communication.[xvii] Our undergraduate degree is the largest major in the School of Liberal Arts and we have graduated more students than anyone in the School in recent years. Our MA program was recognized in 2012 by our National Communication Association as the Outstanding MA program, based on our innovative research, teaching, and mentoring opportunities for graduate students. Clearly it is an exciting time for our program.

Professors in my department hold a variety of research interests beyond health communication. My colleagues study everything from risk communication to organizational conflict to narratives of motherhood, just to name a few. My expertise is in the area of gender and politics. My recent book, *Woman President: Confronting Postfeminist Political Culture*, explores the question of why the US has never elected a woman president. My co-author Karrin Vasby Anderson and I argue that the media narratives that tell the story of political women, specifically during the 2008 US presidential election, demonstrate a significant backlash against the gains that women have made in politics. Instead of positioning women as viable candidates, women are discussed in the media as outsiders, extreme, conniving, and overly-ambitious. We argue that the majority of narratives from public address, television and film, political pop culture, parody, news and Internet media during the 2008 election clustered along this narrative line, creating a storyline that neither Hillary Clinton nor Sarah Palin could overcome. You can read about some of the other academic interests of my faculty colleagues a little later in this essay.

If some of these opportunities at IUPUI sound like interesting choices, then consider studying with us. The School of Liberal Arts offers many scholarship opportunities as you can see here: http://liberalarts.iupui.edu/scholarship/. Our campus offers several exciting scholarship opportunities as well: http://www.iupui.edu/~finaid/services/scholarships/. If you are particularly talented, you might qualify for some of the scholarships offered through the IUPUI Honors College: http://honorscollege.iupui.edu/scholarships/.

What is the Relationship between Academic and Applied Work?

Too often there is the perception that a divide exists between academic research and the applied work of communication practitioners. However, I would argue that 1) academic research is highly valuable to practitioners, and 2) the best academic work is, in fact, applied.

"There is nothing so practical as a good theory," often attributed to Kurt Lewin. Talented communication practitioners know that in order to make good decisions, you must have something to guide you. You can't just go on intuition, observations, or experience alone. Communication theory provides the roadmap for making communication decisions, no matter the situation. Organizational consultants helping their clients manage a crisis would do well to consult the work of William Benoit.

Practitioners working with health organizations in cross-cultural situations to manage risk would benefit by reading Timothy Sellow's work. Individuals and organizations navigating private information should consult the theory of Sandra Petronio. Political consultants working with female politicians could consult my work co-authored with Karrin Vasby Anderson. Academic researchers, by and large, do their work because it makes an impact. It can be applied and has been applied in real world situations. Practitioners, armed with a good theory, are those poised for success.

Certainly clients with whom those practitioners work may not care so much to learn about theory as much as "how can I communicate more effectively." This is really an argument about how the practitioner packages her message to the client. The practitioner makes recommendations to the client, based on theory. The job of the practitioner is to help the client communicate more effectively. The practitioner knows how to do that because she knows her communication theory and can apply it. As a result, academic research is highly valuable to practitioners. This is the kind of applied work that we emphasize at IUPUI.

In our classes, students have the opportunity to work with community-based organizations to help them address communication challenges faced by the organization. Students learn how to apply theory toward solving real world problems and deliver their recommendations to an engaged audience eager to implement their advice. Our students use communication theory to *make better communities*. Their communication *does something*.

Additionally, the best academic work is highly applied. It is a rarity that a communication scholar sits in her office and simply theorizes. The more realistic situation is the communication scholar who sees a problem and sets about solving it. And the results have real world implications. Consider, for example, some of the questions listed above.

My research seeks to answer the research question about reframing the narratives in US political culture in order to see the election of a woman president. It's not simply because I want to theorize about political culture, but I want my theory to do something, to help us get closer to a gender neutral understanding of the presidency. In a similar fashion, my colleague Jonathan Rossing studies racial humor. He is interested in theorizing how humor can provide an opportunity for rhetorical education that can help us engage in conversations about race and racism.

Again, his work is applied with a direct impact on our world. My colleague Jennifer Bute is interested not only in theorizing about how couples manage private information, but in facilitating those conversations to maximize perceptions of social support. Here we have another link between theory and practice. All of this is to say that many academic researchers are driven not by theory itself, but in the applications of that theory to solving a communication problem. Quite frankly, that is where our discipline started. The Ancient Greek rhetoricians saw a problem to address— citizens could benefit from rhetorical skill in order to create a democratic community. In that sense, we really haven't traveled that far from our roots in terms of our applied focus. But the range of questions asked has certainly expanded over the centuries.

Many universities, including IUPUI, have expanded their curriculum to include service learning or civic engagement. This approach is a natural connection to our communication curriculum. Often, classes will partner with an organization in the community who needs assistance with a communication problem that has some connection to the content of the course.

For example, my public communication class assisted a not-for-profit organization in our community who needed a communication plan to attract more attention to its organization and its brand. My students received practical experience in making public communication recommendations and the organization received some good theory-based consulting. IUPUI is often recognized for its community engagement, and this is just one example of how that works in practice.

Chapter 8: Communication & Rhetorical Studies: The Practical Liberal Art of the 21st-Century – Professor Ronald C. Arnett, PhD

Dr Ronald C. Arnett (Ph.D., Ohio University, 1978) is chair and professor of the Department of Communication & Rhetorical Studies and the Henry Koren, C.S.Sp., Endowed Chair for Scholarly Excellence at Duquesne University. He is the author/co-author of nine books, the former editor of Review of Communication, and the current editor of the Journal of Communication and Religion. His recent work, Communication Ethics in Dark Times: Hannah Arendt's Rhetoric of Warning and Hope *(2013, Southern Illinois University Press), won the National* Communication Association's 2013 *Communication Ethics Division's Top Book Award for Philosophy of Communication Ethics. An* Overture to Philosophy of Communication: The Carrier of Meaning *(2013, Peter Lang), co-authored with Annette M. Holba, won the National Communication Association's 2013 Philosophy of Communication division's Best Book Award and the Eastern Communication Association's 2013 Everett Lee Hunt Award. Dialogic Confession: Bonhoeffer's Rhetoric of*

Responsibility (2005, Southern Illinois University Press) received the Eastern Communication Association's 2006 Everett Lee Hunt Award. Communication and Community: Implications of Martin Buber's Dialogue (1986, Southern Illinois University Press) received the Religious Speech Communication Association's 1988 Book of the Year Award. His most recent work is Conflict between Persons: The Origins of Leadership *(2014, Kendall Hunt), co-authored with Leeanne M. Bell McManus and Amanda G. McKendree. Dr. Arnett is the executive director of the Pennsylvania Communication Association and the Eastern Communication Association. His teaching and research interests are in communication and conflict, interpersonal communication, and communication ethics, all of which are infused with philosophy of communication.*

The 20th century was the academic zenith of the field of psychology, with a concentrated focus on understanding the individual psyche that impacted multiple disciplines and professions. The 21st century, however, is the era of communication. The focus of attention moves from therapeutic linkages between and among persons to a complex array of communicative interactions shaped by content, context, perspective, and responsibility.

To be literate as a communication major, one must understand the historical context in which one lives, attending to the questions that define a given place and time—such attentiveness is the beginning of competent communication. Communication is both a theoretical and a practical discipline. Theory offers general insight with practical application addressing local demands between and among communicators—competent communicative interaction thrives on local soil, responding to a general cosmopolitan theoretical insight. This interplay of the theoretical and the practical is manifested in every dimension of the study of communication, from interpersonal to small group to organizational to family communication to mediated communication, and is most aptly represented in studies of communication and culture. In short, the field of communication is the intellectual hub of practical and personal navigation of the 21st century.

21st-Century Study and Practice

Communication is a practical liberal art. The stress on practicality, however, does not suggest simply doing what others have done. The word "practical" is opposed to the notion of routine. A practice requires thoughtful engagement. Routine, on the other hand, lacks consideration of immediate and long-term requirements, needs, and unknown consequences. The communication degree is an exercise in practices of thoughtfulness that constantly attend to local soil. There is no entity called "good communication" in the abstract. Communication majors must learn why discourse shifts and changes from one context to another. The task of communication is to make contact with another, not simply to hear oneself utter familiar sounds. The scope of communication ranges from interpersonal communication study to that of examining culture, questions of media, organizational issues, and communication ethics. Career opportunities for communication majors are abundant because communication is a liberal art that requires one to attend thoughtfully to the uniqueness of a given communicative environment. We cannot prepare students for a fully known future. A communication degree prepares our students to shape the future under conditions of uncertainty.

Unlike some academic programs that lock students into ideas only or, on the other extreme, repetitive acts of technician-like behavior, the communication degree unites application and ideas in thoughtful engagement of practice guided by theory. Such is the crucible of future leadership. Why choose the communication degree? The answer lives within the interplay of theory and application; the communication degree is the thinking degree of creative application in the 21st century.

Communication & Rhetorical Studies at Duquesne University

Our program at Duquesne University begins with the assumption that local soil matters. We built our offerings in response to the vocation of Spiritan priests, a Catholic order known for existential engagement and deep commitment to intercultural missions. Our basic core of classes consists of intercultural communication, communication ethics, the history of communication, communication and technology, and communication and society. Three of our courses are deeply related to our local home: intercultural communication, communication ethics, and the history of communication. The other two courses address significant background information for understanding communication in our time. Communication is not merely a foreground activity. It requires commitment to how and why ideas emerged in the background of a given historical context. Learning about and from history requires one to attend to how others were alert to the world before them, leaving behind conversations of response that might assist us in a new but similar situation.

Investigation of technology and communication in the Department of Communication & Rhetorical Studies at Duquesne University follows the impulse of scholars interested in media ecology. We are interested in the persuasive nature of technology, not merely technology for its own sake, but for understanding the implications of living within a technological world. When does communicative technology assist and when does it unleash harm? We examine society understood as a complex unit that consists of multiple and diverse communities, exploring how communication within a society is quite different than that within an aggregate, a family, or a community. A healthy society invites a diversity of engagements, meeting others within a complex and often contentious public square.

Research within the Department of Communication & Rhetorical Studies at Duquesne University varies from dialogue to communication ethics to the rhetorical implications of technology to an understanding of organizational communication centered on questions of civility, problematic others in the workplace, and the necessity and importance of ensuring spaces for dissent and ongoing questioning within the public domain. Specifically, our program has degrees in integrated marketing communication, corporate communication, communication studies, and rhetoric. The major in integrated marketing communication takes students into the arena of strategic marketplace communication. Those who are interested in working in the business community pursue corporate communication. Communication studies is an individualized degree developed with the guidance of a faculty advisor. The rhetoric major prepares students for graduate school or law school.

Applied Excellence

The field of communication provides opportunities for application in corporate communication. The majors at the Department of Communication & Rhetorical Studies at Duquesne University provide a practical benefit for those interested in corporate communication and integrated marketing communication; students in communication studies and rhetoric are also able to make a move into the marketplace later in their professional development if they so choose. We have relationships with professional firms.

Specifically, our communication complex was built by MARC Advertising and supported by the work of their CEO, Anthony Bucci. Additionally, our communication research has both theoretical and general applications appropriate to a Research I university. Furthermore, we engage in applied research that is relevant to the nonprofit community and local businesses. Most of our classes have an applied component connected to them, uniting theory with practice. We work with real clients in the Pittsburgh area and provide them with research that assists their productivity and the communication ambiance of their enterprises.

Recommendations

We understand communication as a liberal art that appreciates the historical questions before us, and we engage theory that guides the necessity of attending to local communities in the application of any communicative effort. Our contention is that the majority of communicative problems do not rest in the foreground; they rest within the reality of contrasting backgrounds, which consists of ethics and issues, ideas and objectives that matter differently to different communicative interlocutors.

Two books designed specifically to address the background nature of communicative differences emerged from our department: (1) *Communication Ethics Literacy: Dialogue and Difference* (Arnett, Fritz, & Bell, 2009), which examines the complexity of communication ethics in an era of narrative and virtue contention; and (2) *Conflict between Persons: The Origins of Leadership* (Arnett, Bell McManus, & McKendree, 2013), which assumes that many substantial conflicts have ethical roots in different assumptions about what matters. These books address the reality of our contemporary moment and offer suggestions for engaging an era defined by conflict centered on the presupposition that things matter substantially differently to those outside our limited domains of interest and contact.

Interplay of Philosophy of Communication and Rhetoric

The Department of Communication & Rhetorical Studies at Duquesne University works with a philosophical and pragmatic assumption that knowledge of philosophy of communication is essential for communication competence in the 21st century. In an era of the blacksmith, one simply learned a profession that was shaped by common public routine actions. One engaged in those imitative activities until one moved from the status of apprentice to that of journeyman. For many of us, such a world is now only a historical memory. Granted, some people may choose to be a blacksmith today, but in all probability, the choice has little to do with a relative or friend who passes on the craft, but rather emerges from a philosophical conviction that such a series of actions should not be lost and must be preserved by those who continue to care about the craft. Philosophical judgment or a philosophy of communication can be understood as a public standpoint for why we do what we do.

Philosophy of communication is the knowledge/clarity engine for communication in the 21st century. There is no one philosophy of communication; there is no one knowledge/clarity standpoint that one can assume. Philosophy of communication requires one to understand the knowledge/clarity standpoint that propels one's own decision making and practices as well as those of others. This position is akin to Gadamer's (1975/2013) philosophical hermeneutics, which suggests that without bias, information becomes static and lacks innovative possibilities.

Likewise, the insights of Calvin Schrag (1986) unite philosophy of communication and rhetoric through the ineffable action of a "rhetorical turn" that happens when one discovers a "why" or knowledge/clarity standpoint via philosophy of communication. One takes that information, that position, into the public domain, engaging in rhetorical and persuasive action with and toward others. The 21st century returns us to the necessity of knowing why and recognizing that the communication task eventually results in a persuasive effort of convincing oneself and others of a given direction. We understand this interplay of philosophy of communication and rhetoric as integral to all dimensions of communication.

This perspective undergirds our more conventional degrees—communication studies and rhetoric—and is central to our integrated marketing communication and corporate communication degrees that directly engage the marketplace. Richard Bernstein (1983), in his book *Beyond Objectivism and Relativism: Science, Hermeneutics, and Praxis*, contends that we live in a peculiar time in which the philosophical and practical have crisscrossed, meaning that the practical without the philosophical is no longer applicable but is instead antiquated. Having philosophical knowledge/clarity is now a practical necessity in a world of difference. There are few truisms in a postmodern culture, or what many have referred to as a transmodern moment.

Of course difference is central, and for our program understanding the philosophical knowledge/clarity position or standpoint from which one works and others function requires one to recognize an inevitable rhetorical turn as we argue for what matters in the 21st century. Our program is also intensely interested in the importance of communication ethics, as stated earlier. We understand communication ethics as a form of philosophy of communication that has weight; it matters (Cooren, 2010).

Communication ethics has conventionally been framed, particularly in modernity, as a series of agreed upon conventions. In short, from the conventional understanding, the contention is that communication ethics can solve or manage a given issue. This position, however, is tied to a modern presupposition that truth is ascertainable and can be and should be imposed in a given communication environment. The optimism of this perspective assumes that ethics can thoughtfully order a given communication environment.

The downside is that such confidence is an invitation to problematic sins of modernity—colonialism, totalitarianism, and hegemonic control. Our understanding in the Department of Communication & Rhetorical Studies at Duquesne University of communication ethics de-privileges the power of communication ethics, lessening its ability to impose an answer, which maximizes the significance of communication ethics as tied to learning and understanding.

Just as there are multiple philosophy of communication positions, there are multiple communication ethics standpoints. The communicative task of the 21st century is to seek to understand positions that propel one's action and those of others. Communication ethics becomes an essential ingredient for understanding and cannot from this perspective be used as a communicative weapon to declare the other as out of line. Communication ethics are multiple and tied to a series of pragmatic communicative positions and actions that have paradigmatic coherence. By de-privileging the power of communication ethics, we make communication ethics central in all communication that matters, not as a form of resolution or determinism, but as the baseline beginning of understanding one's own position in the world and that of others.

Communication ethics in the 21st century is a form of philosophy of communication that must be taken seriously in one's own life and in our engagements with others. Our department offers a conference on communication ethics every other year. The theme of the conference in 2014 was "Rhetoric and Philosophy of Communication Ethics: Social Justice in Organizations and History." We invited the following six scholars with national and international reputations: Briankle Chang

(University of Massachusetts), François Cooren (Université de Montréal), Gail T. Fairhurst (University of Cincinnati), Annette Holba (Plymouth State University), Ramsey Eric Ramsey (Arizona State University), and Ingrid Volkmer (University of Melbourne).

Additionally, we offer a conference on philosophy of communication in the alternate years, which commenced in 2013. The center of that inaugural conference was the work of Richard Lanigan (1988) and communicology.[1] We select a different theme for the conference every time it is offered, and each theme is focused on communication ethics and philosophy of communication. An edited book has emerged out of a large number of these conferences. The latest edited book, *Philosophy of Communication Ethics: Alterity and the Other* (Arnett & Arneson, in press), emerged from the 2012 communication ethics conference and is being published by Fairleigh Dickinson University Press.

Research Foundation

Just as we consider philosophy of communication

---

[1] Communicology, first introduced by Richard L. Lanigan in 1988, situates semiotic phenomenology within philosophy of communication and human language.

that takes a rhetorical turn essential to every dimension of human communication, we also embrace the necessity of doing research at the undergraduate, graduate, and faculty levels of our department. For instance, one of the requirements of undergraduate assistants, who work with faculty and graduate students, is to complete a research assignment with a graduate student, which will be presented at a local or national conference and potentially be submitted for publication review. This activity is in line with the increasing emphasis on undergraduate research at our university and not only assists our undergraduate students but also offers our graduate students an opportunity to mentor another in research skills and development.

Additionally, graduate students are encouraged to engage in scholarship for conferences and publication. A doctoral degree is a research degree that necessitates outstanding research in order to inform students of important historical and contemporary developments in the field of communication. Faculty members within the department are encouraged to model a commitment to research by spending a considerable amount of time in scholarly endeavors.

For instance, at the 2013 National Communication

Association conference, the department secured three book awards and two outstanding article awards: (1) the Communication Ethics Division's Top Book Award for Philosophy of Communication Ethics for *Communication Ethics in Dark Times: Hannah Arendt's Rhetoric of Warning and Hope* (Arnett, 2013); (2) the Philosophy of Communication Division's award for Best Book for *An Overture to Philosophy of Communication: The Carrier of Meaning* (Arnett & Holba, 2013); (3) the Clifford G. Christians Ethics Research Award from the Carl Couch Center for Social and Internet Research for *Professional Civility: Communicative Virtue at Work* (Fritz, 2013); (4) the Philosophy of Communication Division's Journal Article of the Year award for "Camera as Sign: On the Ethics of Un-concealment in Documentary Film and Video" (Butchart, 2012); and (5) the Franklyn S. Haiman Award for Distinguished Scholarship in Freedom of Expression for "Mapping Free Speech Scholarship in the Communication Discipline: 1969–2006" (Arneson & Dewberry, 2009).

The 21st-century communication student again must understand the uniqueness and application of traditional ideas and novel ideas to unique communicative settings. Such a scholarly palate matures through the practice of doing research. We contend that the 21st century is, indeed, the communication century. Departmentally, the

Department of Communication & Rhetorical Studies at Duquesne University understands this communication century to be centered on three basic coordinates: philosophy of communication, rhetoric, and research sophistication.

An Energized Discipline

Communication and rhetorical studies is a naturally energized field of study. The answers are not solidified, reified, and carved in stone but found in the interplay of historical events, theoretical developments, and contemporary demands that recast and reshape old assumptions into novel, creative applications. Indeed, there is no such thing as good communication. There is, however, a competent communicator in the 21st century. Such a person knows why knowledge matters in a given communicative setting and understands the persuasive character of the weight of such recognition and the consequence of testing ideas through thoughtful research. Communication competence in the 21st century requires ongoing daily acts of research and development, knowledge of theory, and a creative spirit that is ever wary of blind, thoughtless technique. This field of study gathers energy from the fundamental fact that great communication emerges in a given temporal moment, attending to local soil and to all the demands that shape a given place and time.

Works Cited

Arneson, P., & Dewberry, D. R. (2009). Mapping free speech scholarship in the communication discipline: 1969–2006. *Free Speech Yearbook, 43* (199–228).

Arnett, R. C. (2013). Communication ethics in dark times: Hannah Arendt's rhetoric of warning and hope. Carbondale: Southern Illinois University Press.

Arnett, R. C., & Arneson, P. (Eds.) (in press). *Philosophy of communication ethics: Alterity and the Other.* Madison, NJ: Fairleigh Dickinson University Press.

Arnett, R. C., Fritz, J. M. H., & Bell, L. (2009). *Communication ethics literacy: Dialogue and difference.* Thousand Oaks, CA: Sage.

Arnett, R. C., & Holba, A. M. (2013). An overture to philosophy of communication: The carrier of meaning. New York: Peter Lang.

Arnett, R. C., Bell McManus, L., & McKendree, A. G. (2013). *Conflict between persons: The origins of leadership.* Dubuque, IA: Kendall Hunt Publishing

Company.

Bernstein, R. J. (1983). *Beyond objectivism and relativism: Science, hermeneutics, and praxis.* Philadelphia: University of Pennsylvania Press.

Butchart, G. (2012). Camera as sign: On the ethics of unconcealment in documentary film and video. *Social Semiotics, 25* (1–16).

Cooren, F. (2010). *Action and agency in dialogue.* Amsterdam: John Benjamins Publishing Co.

Fritz, J. M. H. (2013). Professional civility: Communicative virtue at work. New York: Peter Lang.

Gadamer, H. G. (2013). *Truth and method.* London: Bloomsbury Academic. (Original work published 1975)
Lanigan, R. L. (1988). Phenomenology of communication: Merleau-Ponty's thematics in communicology and semiology. Pittsburgh, PA: Duquesne University Press.

Schrag, C. O. (1986). *Communicative praxis and the space of subjectivity.* Bloomington: Indiana University Press.

Chapter 9: Nothing So Practical as a Good Theory – Professor Maxwell McCombs, PhD

Professor Max McCombs is internationally recognized for his research on the agenda-setting role of mass communication, the influence of the media on the focus of public attention. Since the original Chapel Hill study with his colleague Donald Shaw coined the term "agenda setting" in 1968, more than 400 studies of agenda setting have been conducted by scholars worldwide. Professor McCombs' book summarizing this research, **Setting the Agenda: The Mass Media and Public Opinion** *(Polity Press, 2004 and 2014), has been described as the Gray's Anatomy of agenda-setting theory. A past president of the World Association for Public Opinion Research and a fellow of the International Communication Association, McCombs has received an honorary doctorate from the University of Antwerp, the Paul J. Deutschmann Award for Excellence in Research from the Association for Education in Journalism and Mass Communication and is the co-recipient with Donald Shaw of the Murray Edelman Award of the American Political Science Association and WAPOR's Helen Dinerman Award. McCombs is the Jesse H. Jones Centennial Chair in*

Communication Emeritus at the University of Texas at Austin and has been a visiting professor annually at the University of Navarra in Spain since 1994. McCombs received his M.A. and his Ph.D. from Stanford University and his B.A. from Tulane University. Prior to joining the University of Texas faculty in 1985, he was on the faculties of Syracuse University, University of North Carolina at Chapel Hill, and U.C.L.A. and immediately after college was a reporter at the New Orleans Times-Picayune.

Many Messages Satisfy Curiosity - Few Make any Real Contribution

Millions of messages are created and distributed every day. Think of how many messages you already have heard on the radio, saw in the newspaper, on television, Twitter, Facebook, and numerous other media today.

Of course, it is a small sample of all the messages that are available. Among those millions of daily messages a substantial number are simply ignored. Many reach only small niche audiences. And of those that reach larger numbers of recipients, many are only casually noted, only a few are closely considered. In the contemporary communication landscape, there is considerable attention to its vastness, the ability of some message to quickly reach extraordinarily large numbers of persons across wide geographic areas.

However, the central question about any message – whether a story by a news organizations or the tweet of an individual – is not the speed and vastness of its distribution. The central question about any message is whether it created awareness and understanding in the recipient. This is where the vast majority of the daily flood of messages falls short. Many messages satisfy curiosity. Few make any real contribution.

This is where the study of communication has great benefit for an individual. Studying communication can create an understanding of the communication process that can be used personally as well as professionally. And this is where theory comes into the picture. Scientific theories are not fanciful conjectures, but rather are intellectual maps and overviews of the various facets of communication based on empirical observation.

In other words, theories are a systematic picture of the communication process and its effects. One of the founders of communication study, Wilbur Schramm, was fond of observing that there is nothing so practical as a good theory – a guide book as one sets about communicating effectively.

Theory is More than an Abstraction, More than just Ideas and Hypotheses

Theory is more than an abstraction, more than just ideas, hypotheses and the intellectual architecture found in books and journal articles. Theory also is a style of thinking, a continuous and on-going probing of areas of interest. This cumulative nature of science and theoretical thinking is particularly apparent in the hard sciences where dozens of elves and a few giants constantly keep chipping away and pushing the frontiers of knowledge forward.

The long-term cumulative results of theories in communication and the other social sciences tend to be more loosely organized, but the long-term cumulative effects can be very similar. Across the last half century, they definitely have been in agenda-setting research, a theory about the role of the news media in focusing public attention and understanding on a few key issues of the day – the initial steps in the formation of public opinion.

In the popular view, the history of advances in science is marked by "discoveries." Charles Goodyear discovered rubber, Jonas Salk discovered a vaccine to prevent polio, and so on. The implication is that these scientists suddenly – perhaps even serendipitously – happened upon something new and wonderful.

Although it is doubtful that there have been very many discoveries in the physical and biological sciences that were not preceded by long periods of study and investigation, it is almost certainly the case in the social sciences that our knowledge of individuals and society accrues incrementally. Through scholarly persistence, the implicit gradually becomes explicit. Studying communication creates an awareness of this process and its results.

Agenda Setting Theory – an Example

This intellectual evolution in which the implicit gradually becomes explicit definitely is the history of agenda-setting theory, which began with a tightly focused study during the 1968 U.S. presidential election (McCombs & Shaw, 1972) and subsequently has gradually evolved into a broad multi-faceted theory of the public communication process (McCombs, 2014).

Our "discovery" of basic agenda-setting effects – the ability of the news media to focus public attention on a short list of issues that came to be regarded by the public as the most important issues of the day – expanded into a second level of agenda-setting effects, attribute agenda setting, the ability of the news media to focus public attention on specific attributes or frames of those issues.

These two effects explicate Walter Lippmann's thesis in his classic *Public Opinion* that the news media are the bridge between "the world outside and the pictures in our heads." Most recently, agenda setting theory and research has moved beyond the influence of the news media on the salience of specific issues and individual attributes of these issues to ask to what extent are the media able to transfer the salience of an integrated picture? Some psychologists and philosophers hold that people's mental representations operate pictorially, diagrammatically or cartographically.

In other words, audiences map out objects and attributes as network-like pictures according to the interrelationships among these elements. From this perspective, the news media transfer the salience of relationships among a set of elements to the public. These sets could be the issues on the media or public agendas or the attributes of these issues on the media or public agendas.

Initial exploration of the extent to which the news media can transfer the salience of relationships among a set of elements to the public focused on the transfer of the salience of political candidates' attributes in two Texas elections from the news media to the public. During the 2012 U.S. presidential election, the relationships among issues in tweets by citizens and by journalists from mainstream and partisan media were examined. Both studies found strong links between the network of elements in the news and the network of these elements among the public. In this new, broader perspective on the bundling of agenda elements – the third level of agenda setting – the focus is on the transfer of the salience of entire networks of objects or attributes, a theoretical advance that yields a more precise map of the pictures in our heads (Guo, 2014).

Two Theoretical Roads

In most fields of research, there are two roads leading to theoretical advances, the road of basic research and the road that begins with practical problems. Advances along either road require intellectual creativity and often begin with simple curiosity. During my time as a graduate student at Stanford University, a member of the physics faculty explained that his celebrated theoretical work on the nature of matter began with a simple thought on his deck one spring afternoon in Palo Alto: Why does a bottle of beer foam when you open it?

The intellectual road of basic research is very familiar. There are many textbooks and famous treatises about the hypothetico-deductive method, Bacon's Idols, and other aspects of the scientific method. Here I will focus on the route of practical problems.

By way of preface, both applied research focused on the practical problems of communication and basic theoretical research are two sides of the same coin. Both seek to inform our understanding and use of communication. What links the two is the necessity of creating meaning for data. The mindless collection of hunches, data and statistics, whether in conjunction with day-to-day activities or from idle academic curiosity, has no value until you create it.

As philosopher of science Carl Hempel once remarked, those who aren't looking for anything in particular seldom find anything in particular. And the broader and more general the scope of your inquiry, the more rigorous and systematic its theoretical base, the greater is the likelihood of finding something of value.

A common narrative regarding the relationship

between theoretical research and practical applications is that theory offers a useful intellectual overview of an area that can help organize decision making about practical matters. In other words, the practical application is a trickle-down by-product of traveling down the theoretical road. But theoretical advances can result from a journey that begins on the road of practical problems. Agenda-setting has its origins on both of these paths.

Walter Lippmann's *Public Opinion* is the intellectual origin of agenda setting theory. But the more immediate origins of this line of agenda setting arose from curiosity about what happens to the impact of news coverage when one event in the news overshadows another. Decisions about how to play news stories have important ethical and practical consequences.

A Short Reading List

To repeat, theory is more than just an intellectual tool. Studying communication can provide you with basic knowledge about the major theories, but theory also is a way of thinking systematically and strategically about communication. Books and articles detailing specific communication theories can be useful blueprints in the construction of messages – whatever the topic or purpose. More importantly, thinking theoretically can take you beyond the specific blueprints and enhance the effectiveness of your communications.

References

Guo, L. (2014). Toward the third level of agenda setting theory: A Network Agenda Setting Model. In T. Johnson (Ed.), *Agenda setting in a 2.0 world: New agendas in communication*. New York: Routledge.

Lippmann, W. (1922). *Public Opinion*. Macmillan, New York.

McCombs, M. (2014). Setting the Agenda: Mass Media and Public Opinion. Polity Press, Cambridge, UK.

McCombs, M. & Shaw, D. (1972). The agenda-setting function of mass media. *Public* Opinion Quarterly, 69, 176–187.

Chapter 10: An Important Part of your Education to Work in the Communication Field Happens Outside of the Classroom – Professor César García, PhD

Dr César García is an Associate Professor of public relations and Chair of the Communication Department at Central Washington University (CWU). He specializes in teaching and research on public relations and public opinion. He has more than a decade of experience in Europe in the professional world of public relations for international firms such as Edelman and Pleon. César has written numerous articles in international academic publications such as Public Relations Review, Journal of Communication Management, Public Relations Journal, and International Journal of Strategic Communication, among others. He believes in the interdependence of culture and communication. For that reason, he co-created a study-abroad program titled "Communication and Culture in Spain" where his students had the opportunity to meet communication professionals from other countries and visit PR firms, newspapers and TV stations. He truly believes that an active involvement in the public sphere helps foster a better understanding of the field of public communication. He is a regular contributor to Spain's version of The Huffington Post (http://www.huffingtonpost.es/cesar-garcia/) as a result of his intellectual work outside of academia. In his blog, César writes about topics that range from education and communication to politics. He has published three books: American Psique (2011); History of a stereotype. Spanish intellectuals in the United States (1885-1936) (2009), and Public opinion in Santayana (2006). César García is also the author of the first translation of Walter Lippmann's classic The Phantom Public for Spanish-speaking audiences.

Communication is a Perfect Field to Vehicle any Passion you may Have

These days, the field of communication for a number of students has to do with new information technologies. Terms such as video or printed journalism sound obsolete to them. For the most part, students want to study a degree in a communication field (which at CWU is public relations, journalism, film and video studies, and communication studies) to find a job. A number of them feel attracted to the idea of working in a professional field with a high level of human interaction and in which they can be relatively successful without a strong hard skills component.

They are right in the sense that it is not only media organizations which need communication specialists these days. Any company, non-profit, educational or government institution creates content to meet the expectations of their audiences or stakeholders. In a noisy world where attention is even scarcer than money, catching a portion of attention through communication strategies and techniques have became a challenge for many organizations. Giving a variety of customized choices on content through a variety of channels is an imperative for success. It is a trendy field but not new at all, because the need to tell good stories to viewers, listeners, readers, clients and workers was always there. It was, however, considered a more intuitive endeavor that could be capitalized by a few. Nowadays, every person or organization aspires to become a good storyteller.

I always tell my students that communication is a perfect field to vehicle any passion that they may have. If you like cars, you can do advertising for a car company, write a blog or press reviews about cars, film a car race or work in the human resources department of a car manufacturer. I think this merging of academic knowledge and private passion is one of the keys of success of the communication field. You can move across a number of professional fields with a set of similar skills and knowledge.

Students also feel motivated working for a field without borders where the international factor is only getting stronger year after year, that helps them to relate better with people from other cultures, and with an increasing vocation for entertainment that they don't see in, perhaps, more technical or purer humanistic disciplines.

And last, but not least, there is an experiential factor. When you study communication, you learn doing, experiencing, generating final products, which does not happen in many other fields. In CWU's Communication Department, there is hardly a student who graduates without having worked in at least one of our media outlets, which include a printed and online newspaper, an online magazine, a TV station, and a PR/Advertising agency. Our film students make movies and write scripts. When students finish our programs, they always have a portfolio to show to their future employers and, what is more important, they feel confident about their capabilities because they have used them and created an end product. This sort of experiential learning is less common in other disciplines.

How can Practitioners Benefit from Academic Research?

We live in a data-driven society, so research is fundamental in any aspect regarding the academic and/or the professional world. There is a common misunderstanding that tends to identify academic research with scholarship only.

In our program, we have a number of classes in research (media research, advertising research) and we integrate a research component into almost all our classes. You cannot work in the communication field if you don't know your audiences or how the public perceives your content. This applies to advertising, PR or TV. And for this reason, we constantly encourage our students to do applied research. We also think that universities should use research on behalf of communities. For example, recently our PR students implemented the broadest-ever survey for the local Downtown Association as a touchstone for implementing new efforts to keep transforming downtown.

Regarding scholarship research in communication, I personally see a disconnect between a number of subjects that are investigated in academic journals and the professional world and society as whole. It seems that in terms of time frame (academic journals' processes are very slow and bureaucratic in part due to the fact that there is no monetary reward for peer-reviewers and many of them are still printed journals), subject relevance, and a lack of market drive, academic research is in a situation of disadvantage. In a number of cases, research published in journals lacks the immediacy due to these long processes.

For example if you write on sport communication you may publish an article when the coaches or players you've written about are no longer on the same teams. In these cases, research does not become irrelevant but certainly the immediacy would have generated more interest. Good research does not have to compete with journalism, but in applied fields such as communication, it does need to evolve to meet the expectations of professionals.

Another problem is that, unfortunately, sometimes scholars just care about having an empirically-based publication, leaving aside if the topic is important or not. It happens with more frequency than it should that substance is sacrificed for the benefit of the methodology.

The positive side is, of course, that academic research tends to be more independent and sometimes addresses important topics, with social meaning, that otherwise the market would never pay attention to. For instance, we increasingly know more about the effects of media on kids. If these types of studies were implemented by private firms, there would be less control and probably more manipulation.

In any case, I would say that a strong academic/scholarship background helps you in your professional career even if you do not want to become a university professor. The President of CWU, a former public relations practitioner and scholar, recently told me how useful his ability to read survey data from his times as a scholar are now that he has to make executive and monetary decisions.

Benefits of Online Education

A main communication education trend in the USA these days is the cultivation of experiential learning. I think that, in this sense, the old division between research and teaching universities concerning communication education is becoming smaller. It is true that there are still some research universities with high endowments and donors that give more priority to research in communication, but even these universities increasingly care about their students having a hands-on education through their work in media outlets, internships, practicum, etc...

Distance education, through multimodal learning, is also growing considerably because it allows an expansion of the market to reach populations otherwise limited because of time or geographical constraints. New education technologies offer the possibility of developing customized programs with a high level of interaction between student and professor and in which students can be even more accountable than in a class setting. This modality of education as well generates a higher return of investment for universities that can, at the same time, be reinvested in on-campus education.

This trend does not seem to be going as fast as it could, but I predict that in 10 years there will be very few US universities not offering at least 20-25 percent of their courses this way. If in the future, students of a course called History of German Cinema can have instantaneously available online the 15 movies that they need to see and discuss for that class, I see a clear advantage of the online method over the face-to-face class that force them to make sometimes undesirable choices in terms of jobs to pay for their education. American campuses these days are full of students that take face-to-face and distance education classes at the same time.

Having said that, my opinion is that the communication programs that aspire to be perceived as top range will still be offering a majority of their classes on-campus, will still have an important number of tenure-track professors instead of mostly professionals among their faculty, and certainly will take care about the research factor regarding faculty and students.

$80,000 for a Keynote Speech if you can Connect with the Business World!

My main tip for future or current communication studies is always the same and, in a number of ways, may sound paradoxical: the most important part of your education is you: what kind of person you are, and your level of curiosity about what is going on in the world. In a way, an important part of your education to work in the communication field happens outside of the classroom.

I just read an interview with Malcolm Gladwell where he talks about his ability to connect with the business world (and charge $80,000 per conference) although he does not know much about business. The professional world is looking for people who can identify and anticipate trends, among them communication trends that help to establish emotional connections with different audiences. The only way to do that is to maintain a high level of curiosity about the world: being on top of current affairs, travelling, meeting people that are not necessarily like you, attending events, trying new foods, etc... A good communication program should build an environment that stimulates students' curiosity.

My experience is that people who enjoy life more know the world better and understand new trends. And this, for sure, applies to the field of communication.

Chapter 11: Communication Studies – Professor Richard Letteri, PhD

Richard Letteri is Professor and Chair of Communication Studies at Furman University. He teaches courses in discourse theory, political communication, media criticism and film studies. He also directs a study aboard program in Italy where he teaches a course in the public spaces of classical and Renaissance Italy. He has published articles on American and Chinese film in such journals as Quarterly Review of Film and Video, Asian Studies, and Global Studies. Presently, he is working on comparative studies of Italian and Chinese film.

Preparing Students for Careers in Communication

As the Communication Studies website declares, "Since the Greek *paideia* and the Renaissance *studia humanitas,* the study of the historical and social character of communication has been fundamental to higher learning." Not only does our department investigate the ways in which oral and written texts — both ancient and modern — communicate and persuade, we also explore how new technologies influence interpersonal and mass communication and affect our sense of who we are as individuals and a society.

To understand fully how we integrate the study of rhetoric and new media into our curriculum, how our department's pedagogic goals are furthered through student research, internships, clubs, and study abroad programs, and how successful we have been in preparing students for further academic study or careers in communication, we need to consider first the academic needs of our majors and the nature of Furman University as a liberal arts college.

Although our students may have taken a course in public speaking in high school, participated in a debate program, or surfed the Web and interacted with others on some form of social media, they still need to develop fundamental skills in creating oral, written, and visual texts. Likewise, the vast majority of our students come to us without sufficient knowledge in basic areas of world history, political economy, society, and culture. Still fewer have studied the methods of critical analysis of oral, print, and visual texts.

Four Requirements of a Communication Major

As a liberal arts college, Furman University mandates a series of general educational requirements that exposes students to a variety of disciplines, histories, and cultures in order to widen and sharpen their critical understanding of the world and their place within it. Many of the courses in our department's curriculum fulfill the university's requirements. To this extent, these courses provide either an interdisciplinary or discipline-specific perspective on the role communicative practices play in history, politics, society, and culture.

Unlike many large universities (and most small ones, too), we do not separate the study of rhetoric and mass communication into distinct tracks within our department. Rather, we believe it is vital that students are aware of the principles, techniques, theories, and methodologies for the production and critical understanding of texts in both fields. Hence, our major has four requirements: two practical courses in public speaking and digital communication where students examine and put into practice the main principles, strategies, and techniques for creating oral and digital texts; and two courses which introduce students to the main theories, concepts, issues, and events in the fields of rhetoric and mass communication. Students can further advance their rhetorical and media skills in the areas of argumentation, print journalism (offered within the English Department), broadcast communication, and advocacy.

In addition, we offer many upper-level courses in the history of public address and the mass media, ancient and modern rhetoric, the political economy of the mass media, communication law, political communication and the public sphere, media criticism and the methods of semiotics, psychoanalytic film theory, Marxism, cultural studies and post-colonialism, international communication, African-American and women's rhetoric, Italian and African film, and qualitative and quantitative methods of mass media research.

Emphasis on Communication Skills and Summer Research Stipends

With many of these courses, students can, on the one hand, study quantitative and qualitative research methods that will provide them with fundamental skills for analyzing data obtained through polls, focus groups, and interviews — which are some of the main ways professional organizations collect information on their clients and constituents — while on the other hand, study methods for the close reading of speeches and arguments, film and television images, and various digital images so that they will be able to construct, analyze, and criticize new texts and images in any professional field.

The department also offers a variety of opportunities for students to develop their skills and understanding of communication through student-faculty research, internships, study abroad programs, and student clubs. With respect to student research at the undergraduate level, we are very cautious not to stress research over the study of communication specifically and the humanities, social sciences, and communication technology more generally. As previously mentioned, students usually come to college with an inadequate background in the humanities and science and have very few technical skills related to public speaking, media production, and digital communication. Hence, most of their undergraduate education should focus upon these areas of study.

Moreover, as part of a liberal arts institution, neither faculty nor student research is a top priority. However, we do offer courses where students conduct research independently or under faculty guidance. Furman University even offers a stipend of approximately $3000 for faculty-led summer research. Students have researched the history of broadcasting in South Carolina, the use of cell phones and other technology by market women in Ghana, print media documentation of American public address in the 19th and 20th centuries, and the principles, strategies, and techniques of classical and contemporary public speaking, which led to the publication of my textbook, *A Handbook of Public Speaking* (2002).

Internships at Local, National, and International Institutions

The department also offers internships at local, national, and international institutions, both public and private. Students work in television newsrooms, for newspapers and magazines, at social media outlets, and in public relations firms or departments in major corporations. Many also sharpen their communicative skills advocating for non-profit organizations, non-government organizations, and politicians and political parties.

Some students travel abroad to take classes and work as interns for the Scottish Parliament in Edinburgh, or the European Union in Brussels, Belgium. Others take part in study groups that travel through Turkey, Greece, and Italy learning how societies from the ancient Greeks to the Italian Fascists employed art, architecture, and public space to reflect their ruling ideologies. Closer to campus, students continue to hone their communicative skills by participating in the student-run news station *FUTV*, the student newspaper, *The Paladin*, and the Debate Society and Mock Trial.

We intend to provide our majors first with the fundamental skills for creating informative, persuasive, and aesthetically effective texts, have them study the main theories, methods, and issues related to oral, print, electronic, and digital communication, and then offer them ways to polish their skills and understand the political, ethical, and social consequences of the real-world applications of those skills. Students can also expand both their understanding and practical knowledge of communicative practices through various extra-curricular opportunities.

How Successful is this Pedagogic Strategy?

One might rightly ask, "How successful is this pedagogic strategy?" Although we do not collect information regularly on our graduates, they have a very good track record in finding jobs shortly after graduation in a diverse set of fields. Even since the 2008 recession, many majors have begun careers in broadcast and print journalism, public relations and marketing, and business and non-profit organizations within three months of graduating. A small percentage of our majors go on to graduate work in communication, but most who decide to continue their education go on to law school.

Finally, as more and more companies, organizations, and agencies turn to social media and other forms of digital communication to address clients and customers, many of our graduates find work in professional communication agencies. We have found that our curricular and extra-curricular emphasis on the study and practice of journalism, broadcast communication, digital communication, public speaking, argumentation, advocacy, and other modes of communication offer students a variety of skills that are applicable to jobs in business, government, and advocacy, as well as the integrated media platforms of organizations both large and small.

Chapter 12: An internship or Practicum in the Industry is Critical – Professor Even Culp, Ed.D.

Dr. Even Culp is a storyteller who creates documentary films. His film making has taken him from the foothills of Georgia to the plains of Kansas exploring Cherokee culture. The four programs in this series introduced him to several outstanding artists, leading to another series on Native American artists. These two documentary series were awarded multiple Tellys, a national award given for a non-broadcast educational program. Of great benefit, students served as directors, associate producers and crew members for the series, providing them with invaluable experience. Even's latest documentary effort shares the experiences of a Pearl Harbor survivor. At ORU, Even mentors students serving in industry internships: advertising, marketing, journalism, web development, broadcasting, film and TV production and sound mixing/recording. He enjoys other cultures, and his capstone class, Campaign Strategies, partners teams of senior students with real-world clients to solve basic problems in developing nations. After students complete the basic research, they produce a media package to communicate the problem and solution to a funding organization. Even is always amazed

*at the creativity and inventiveness students bring
to these projects. Students literally are changing
the world using their talents and skills in
communication arts. Most recently, Dr. Culp
created and now directs the Center for Faculty
Excellence at Oral Roberts University. He
coordinates University-wide academic efforts in
the following areas in faculty development and co-
leads initiatives in the University's online
curriculum.*

Why Study Communication?

The study of communications and its applications
is a broad spectrum since all human beings
communicate in some form across multiple
mediums. Typical academic communications
departments may range in practical offerings from
the fine arts-art, theater, dance, debate,
organizational and interpersonal communication,
public relations, advertising, marketing, social
media, television production, film and radio. There
is also the area of audiology and speech pathology
which addresses abnormality in the human body as
they relate to communication challenges. The
theoretical studies cover a broad gambit as well.

Some focus on the individual and getting their
needs met through such studies as media

gratification; others focus on systems such as general systems theory. A large body of work is been done in communications and psychology dealing with intrapersonal and interpersonal communication. In the theology and communication area much as been studied relate to communication with one's God and the role of prayer and meditation in one's life.

An undergraduate degree in communication links a strong foundation for the student to understand oneself, the communication systems of the world and the media forces that influence our decisions. Most undergraduate degrees also have a component of applied skills to prepare the student for a job market. At the advanced level, masters or doctorate students usually narrow the scope of their focus in either research or applied skills.

Undergraduate Research and Scholarships

Undergraduate research and prepare students if there are interested in advanced degree. It also teaches him the process of evaluating primary and secondary research/information. In this age of a glut of information, it is critical that students be able to assess the sources and validity of information. Only through this process can knowledge he discerned and wisdom obtained. Without adequate research and appropriate assessment of analytics, businesses and individuals can take actions based on faulty information. These actions can cause a loss of revenues or impact the effectiveness of a specific intervention or relationship.

Scholarships at Oral Roberts University are primarily focused on the whole person scholarship program which seeks to encourage recruitment of students interested in developing the components of body, mind, and spirit. These elements would lead to a student who is professionally competent, capable of articulating themselves both verbally and written and be a leader in their field. http://www.oru.edu/quest/#sthash.HQUF1pMv.d pbs my present research interest on the effective strategies of delivering instruction at a distance. There is a rush by many universities to embrace online education but many are utilizing practices which are ineffective and not been tested.

Difference Between Theoretical Research and Practical Research

There are those who are less interested in research as they are into the practical arts in developing their craft. Theoretical research often gives us a new paradigm in which to look at a set of interactions or relationships between different components. Practical research often indicates what strategies might be more effective for what elements need to be eliminated to increase efficiencies. All communicators are interested in being more effective in their task or goals.

At Florida State University, based on a theoretical model, I was involved in the research of study of speech anxiety. Students would give speeches while wired to passive electrodes where we took various body measurements of heart rate and perspiration. This research was gathering raw data of a firsthand nature. The findings then allowed researchers to try various techniques to either reduce speech anxiety or use it more effectively in the delivery of meaningful oral presentations. So in this case, the research started in the laboratory, but developed into practical applications for each of us who have to speak in front of groups from time to time. Research provides information which can guide these practices and decisions.

My own doctoral research looked at what media students gravitate towards to resolve issues of loneliness or in the quest to seek companionship. Was it feature-length movies, TV, social media, gaming, etc. knowing where people look to get their needs satisfied helps inform the producers of content, how they might better shape their message or product. This body of research has been called media gratifications. Since various media, channels, can deliver various forms content (handheld devices can now deliver movies, games, social media, television and other personal communication). The research has moved from looking at channels to more specifically looking at content and messages.

The most practical forms of research and the communication area would be in the area of marketing. Students need to be engaged in courses or internships where real research is on-going. Focus groups and questionnaires about consumer preferences are critical to advertising campaigns, product placement and messages crafted for specific demographics, i.e. healthy food choices targeted to women (mothers) ages 25 to 40. Such research informs the marketer on delivering the message to the appropriate audience in thereby increasing sales and market share. There is great value to students to understand the *processes* of marketing research. The skills bring added value to the new graduate and make them more appealing and competitive in the job market. Some communication majors shy away from the business aspects of communication, preferring the artistic aspects of our industry.

However, whether it's art, film, or interpersonal communication all have a potential value, if they find the right audience. Effective research and marketing bring the artist and the potential consumer together, allowing the artist to continue their craft while satisfying the wants and needs of a segment of the buying public.

Tips for your Success

For the undergraduate is important to get involved in communication early. An internship or practicum in the industry is critical to see where one might have interest in areas where they might develop skills. Faculty should involve students at an early point in their college career with industry.

Within the ORU Communication Arts and Media Department, Students are required to take at least one of the internships during their undergraduate experience. Students may take as many as three across their four years of college. This allows students to explore different professions and see where they might best utilize their skills.

Internship should not be credit for work. A clearly set of objective should be laid out as to what the student will learn and specific outcomes as to how their skills will be enhanced. They must be paired with a mentor who has at least 5 to 10 years of experience in the field the student plans to enter.

Besides the fieldwork, students attend the weekly one-hour class to accomplish several objectives. First, they go through a detailed self-assessment of their strengths and interest, as well as an assessment of various industry professions to match the student with possible career paths and their abilities.

Second, students have been several weeks "packaging" themselves so they possess the appropriate methods by which they might present themselves and their abilities. These methods include the development of a resume, cover letter, interview profile, interview skill sets, polished LinkedIn account and professional dress standards. Next, students research and evaluate what professional organizations they should join to enhance their knowledge and begin networking within the industry.

Finally, students are required to build a set of personal/professional skill sets which include a life statement, developing goals and objectives, demonstration of effective time management, and training and assessment of their financial planning.

These activities clarify the student's interest and what potential professions would be an appropriate match for them. The student then creates their own self promotion to communicate what they're capable of doing. Students also journal and provide a reflection paper on their experience, as well as comment on the management of people and the handling of crisis in the workplace.

Since current students will become manager one day, it's important they intentionally form strong management skills early on. The networking and life skills will serve the students, the balance of their life. These are the required experiences and skill sets students go through within the University's internship program.

Chapter 13: Why Study Communication?: A Difficult Question to Answer – Professor Alec Hosterman, PhD

Dr Alec R. Hosterman is a Senior Lecturer in the Communication Arts program at IU South Bend. He holds an M.A. in Speech Communication from Ball State University and a B.A. in Communication Studies from Aquinas College. Currently, Alec is pursuing a Ph.D. in Technical Communication and Rhetoric from Texas Tech University, focusing on the rhetoric of hyperreality, new media, graphic novels, and comics theory. He keeps a blog about this topic and others related to his research: www.alechosterman.com/WordPress. In 2001, Alec joined the Communication Arts faculty full time, teaching courses in Visual Communication, Comics and Graphic Novels, Argumentation, Deception, Communication Theory, Rhetoric, and Public Relations. As a natural extension of his teaching, Alec serves the Michiana community by giving seminars in deception and identity theft to local non-profit agencies. Prior to teaching, Alec worked in the public relations and marketing department Playing Mantis, Inc., a Michiana-

based national toy manufacturer. There, he worked on the company website, wrote press releases and web copy, performed digital photography, and worked on special event coordination.

"Why study communication?" is, ironically, a difficult question to answer. On the surface it might not seem like that. A stock answer could be "because you can do most anything you want with a degree in communication", which is true to some extent. Granted, one can't actually become a brain surgeon, astronaut, or accountant with a BA or BS in Communication, but they can work *with* surgeons, astronauts, or accountants in many other aspects.

Communication studies and practices what humans do everyday. In fact, we study what people do at least 75% of the day. We speak and write well, think critically about the media we come in contact with, understand how people function in groups, prepare effective presentations, adapt to different situations, and more. And I guess this is why it is so difficult to answer why one should study communication. It really depends on how you view the world around you and what you want to be in that world.

There are Four Abilities that you should Excel at

But in my opinion, there are four abilities that students studying communication should excel at: speaking, writing, thinking, and adapting.

Speaking Well – Students *must* be able to speak well. And this doesn't mean always having something to say. No. It means understanding how words affect audiences, how to structure your argument effectively, and how to vocally conquer the audience waiting to hear you. Speaking well is an art that is improved through practice and experience; don't shy away from doing it. Being articulate and descriptive speaks (no pun intended) to one's character and reputation, one of the most important things that we posses. So practice, practice, and practice even more.

Writing Well – Numerous company surveys have shown that potential employers are looking for candidates that are strong writers. Writing well shows an attention to detail and the ability to manage word choice to reach your end goal. And like speaking, writing is something that doesn't always come naturally to people. Writing like one speaks is *not* effective writing. Practice writing and editing whenever you get the chance – from formal

essays to the e-mails you send to your parents
telling them how you're doing in college.

Thinking Critically – Communication students
should be able to discriminately analyze situations,
apply standards critically, seek out information
from reputable sources, logically reason through
arguments, and predict action based upon the
information at hand. Thinking critically may seem
more like common sense than a skill, but it is
something that will allow you to become a more
well-rounded communicator in the end.

Adapting to Contexts – One's ability to adapt to
various situations is a sign of a cognitively complex
individual. Students assess what the situation calls
for and acts accordingly. They understand how
audiences function and what situation calls for
what type of words. In other words, adaption is
about being fluid in varying contexts.

Opportunities and Career Paths Open to you

When you look at these skills and the overall
discipline that one might think of as
communication, you find a myriad of opportunities
and career paths open to students, especially given
the digital age in which we live. Here are just a few
areas that are popular among graduates:

- *Public Relations* – public information officer, special event coordinator, media analyst, publicist
- *Advertising* – creative director, account manager, media planner, copywriter, marketing director
- *Social Media* – app designer, social media strategist, activism, web designer
- *Sales* – sales representative, recruiter, admissions counselor
- *Human Resources* – mediator, office manager, training and development, counselor
- *Politics* – speech writer, campaign manager, mediator, international relations
- *Journalism* – reporter, newscaster, producer, videographer, blogger
- *Visual Communication* – web designer, creative director, graphic designer
- *Education* – high school speech teacher, college professor, debate coach
- *Technical Communicator* – technical copywriter, researcher, document designer
- *Non-Profit Industry* – community leader, fundraiser, grant writer, lobbyist
- *Entertainment Industry* – actor, game designer, agent

Two Things a Perspective Research Students should Think About

For anyone looking to pursue communication primarily as a research degree, I would encourage him/her to think about two things:

What is the existing body of knowledge on a subject? What kind of research has already been done? What are landmark essays in the field? What is being done currently? Do your research about the field to find out if it is the right fit for your academic curiosity. You wouldn't buy a car without finding out how good of a reputation it is, right? This is no different.

In doing your research, you'll find a corpus of material that comes not just from communication scholars but also sociologists, anthropologists, psychologists, and so forth. Here is one of the benefits of studying communication: we work across different fields because communication, as an object, is inherently linked to other human actions. For instance, telling a lie is not just a communicative event but also a psychological and ethical act.

In the early days of the discipline, communication relied heavily on works already published in psychology, sociology, linguistics, and so forth. As a result, communication research is known as an adventure in cross-disciplinary scholarship. In short, there is an extensive body of knowledge available for us to draw on, both unique to the communicative scholar but also to other tangential fields. Don't be afraid to branch out beyond and see the long-lasting implications for communication scholarship.

What can I offer that body of knowledge? In understanding the intricate ties that communication scholarship has to other disciplines, you should ask yourself what you can contribute to the discipline.

There are two roads one can take in research: theoretical scholarship or applied scholarship (sometimes called praxis). Both types of scholarship are systematic inquiry based upon research questions and/or hypotheses. However, theoretical scholarship asks questions and challenges what it is we know and have come to understand. Generally, this kind of theory is used to interpret what happened, explain how something works, and predict what will happen.

Different theoretical "lenses" allow for different theoretical interpretations. In other words, if you change how you look at an event you'll get a different understanding of it. With this, contribution to theoretical research asks new questions in light of current economic, political, social, or media trends. It poses both practical and hypothetical situations and deepens what it is we know.

Applied scholarship is more pragmatic in scope. Sometimes called praxis (enacting theory by putting it into practice), applied research uses the results of the scholarship to enact or improve existing practices. For example, communication educators might study ways to improve teaching on-line and offer suggestions to create more meaningful dialogue. Or public relations practitioners might benefit from research on the ways users react to apologies offered by business leaders. This knowledge will help them craft more meaningful apologies in the future.

In so far as IU South Bend is primarily a teaching institution, the body of scholarship produced by the Communication Studies faculty is a blend of both theoretical and applied research: some faculty work on extending the discussions of race and gender in international media, while others work on the praxis of members in the health care industry. Likewise, all faculty are engaged in the Scholarship of Teaching and Learning (SoTL). We are about improving our teaching techniques, taking both theoretical and applied research and integrating it into our classroom pedagogy (teaching techniques).

Best Practice Tips

Communication has a history that is as old as human culture. The Hindu religion has a goddess of speech and learning, Saraswati. The Egyptians used the images and icons of hieroglyphics as their primary means of communicating. Similarly, the Greeks and Romans studied rhetoric as a means of developing citizenship and a foundation for persuading the masses in politics and law. What we know about the communication act is really a culmination of 3,000 years of asking questions, observing people, and practicing this cherished art.

If you are interested in pursuing an education in communication, make sure to get a strong foundation first. Practice your speech-making skills. Study how and why we persuade one another. Think about the world from another's perspective. Write, write, and write some more. Argue constructively. Consume media in numerous forms. Seeing how foundational skills work their way in and throughout all forms of human interaction makes you a well-rounded student.

And don't just think these are the only areas to study. Not in the least. Communication is breaking ground in new fields every year. For instance, we also study communication that occurs in virtual environments and online. Some scholars work in game studies while others read and work with comics or graphic novels. Interested in culture? Check out work being done in LGBT or the international scene.

Regardless of what area you study, remember that it's about messages and audiences. Creating messages that reach and affect audiences is what we're all about. From a simple classroom presentation with PowerPoint presentation to an address at the United Nations televised on CNN, powerful and memorable communications begin by understanding who the audience is and what are the best ways to reach them.

Chapter 14: Some Thoughts on Communication and Media Studies – David Hesmondhalgh

*David Hesmondhalgh is Professor of Media, Music and Culture in the School of Media and Communication at the University of Leeds, where he was Head from 2010 to 2013. He is the author (with Kate Oakley, David Lee and Melissa Nisbett) of **Culture, Economy and Politics: the Case of New Labour** (Palgrave, 2015), **Why Music Matters** (Wiley-Blackwell, 2013), **Creative Labour: Media Work in Three Cultural Industries** (Routledge, 2011, co-written with Sarah Baker) and **The Cultural Industries**, now in its third edition (Sage, 2013). He is also editor or co-editor of seven books and journal special issues, including The Media and Social Theory (with Jason Toynbee, Routledge, 2008) and (with Anamik Saha) a special issue of the journal Popular Communication on "Race, Ethnicity and Cultural Production" (2013).*

Universities Need to Be About Much More than Vocational Training

The prospects for communication and media studies as an academic discipline are mixed. This is now a thriving area of research and teaching, and has grown hugely over the last twenty years. But many students understand its purpose in a particular way: as providing vocational training for people who wish to work in occupations such as journalism, public relations, advertising or even strange new jobs such as "event planning".

I believe that universities need to be about much more than vocational training - though there is surely a place for some element of this. Universities should inculcate in students intellectual skills that would allow them to work in a vast range of occupations and professions. Students need to understand what constitutes a valid argument and what does not; what constitutes appropriate and substantial evidence and what does not; and how to convey complex ideas as lucidly and concisely as possible.

Communication is important as an academic discipline – by "discipline" I mean an area of knowledge with established but constantly evolving procedures and topics of enquiry - not because it can provide vocational training for ambitious young people, but because it is an absolutely central aspect of our lives as human beings, and therefore potentially as good a topic as literature or history or geography or sociology for students to study while learning the above intellectual skills.

The Role of Technology

Similarly, technologies of mediated communication ("the media") are transforming the way we communicate, and the way we live, just as they have for the last 100, 500, 5000 years. So I believe that we can't understand the world without understanding communication and the media, and that everyone should study the communication and media at some point in their education, just as everyone should study literature, or art, or music, or history, if only for a little while.

Of course, not everyone will want to specialise in communication and media. But it's perfectly appropriate that a small group of students (say, 1 or 2 per cent of the total university population?) should take a version of media and communication studies as a major or minor. And as part of a degree in those subjects, there should be reflection on what constitutes good communication, including how people's lives might be made better by good professional communicators – whether journalists, film-makers, or web designers.

That way, communication and media education

might contribute to the world by ensuring that those with a particular interest in communication, who might presumably be therefore most likely to want to enter into occupations centred on communication, take seriously the idea that they should contribute to human well-being and not just to their own.

Music and What It Tells Us About Communication

One of my own specialist areas of research and teaching is music as communication. My own recently published book *Why Music Matters* discusses the contribution that music can make to enhancing people's lives, at four levels: at the level of our individual selves, in terms of how music can serve to enhance our understanding of our own lives; in terms of how music might enhance our experience of the most intimate relations between other people, those involving love and sex; in terms of experiences of life-enhancing sociability, within the same space and time (for example, at concerts, parties, festivals and so on); and in terms of experiences of solidarity and communality across time and space, for example when people who have never met, and never will meet, come to be aware of the same music through the power of media technologies, such as recording and digital sharing. Across all four of these "levels" or dimensions, a common theme is music's especially strong relationship to the emotions.

However, the book does not offer a simple celebration of these positive aspects of music. It also shows how these capacities of music to make our lives better are limited as well as enabled by certain features of modern societies. Especially important here is inequality and injustice, and the way in which those societies are fractured by class, ethnic, gender and other divisions. The book reflects my belief that communication and media can only be adequately studied by drawing upon other disciplines too, including sociology, philosophy, musicology and psychology.

My Message to Students

In response to the question posed by the editors, my message to students who are interested in communication, media and music would be as follows. Don't assume that knowing the newest developments is the most important thing; don't believe people who tell you that everything is changing, and that therefore everything that happened before the year 2000 (or whatever) is irrelevant; and look for wisdom as much as for information.

Chapter 15: Communication as a Calling and a Career – Professor Stephen J. Hartnett, PhD

Dr Stephen John Hartnett is Professor and Chair of the Department of Communication at The University of Colorado Denver and the 2nd Vice President of the National Communication Association. For the past 23 years, Hartnett has been teaching in, writing about, and working for change at America's prisons. He has taught college classes and poetry workshops in prisons and jails in Indiana, Illinois, Michigan, Texas, California and Colorado, and has facilitated workshops, participated on panels, and given lectures against the death penalty in 28 states. His commentary on these subjects has appeared in Salon, AlterNet, In These Times, and others, and on MSNBC and over 100 radio stations. In recognition of this work, he has received numerous awards, including the Northwest Communication Association's 2008 Human Rights Award, the University of Colorado's 2010 Thomas Jefferson Award, and CU Denver's 2014 Service Excellence Award. Hartnett is the author or editor of 8 books and dozens of publications related to democracy, social justice, prisons, globalization and empire, and the death penalty. His most recent books include the two-volume **Executing Democracy: Capital**

Punishment & the Making of America, which won the Karlyn Kohrs Campbell Prize in Rhetorical Criticism, and his edited ***Challenging the Prison-Industrial Complex: Activism, Arts, and Education Alternatives***, which won a PASS (Prevention for a Safer Society) Award from the National Council on Crime and Delinquency.

Work your Ways into Satisfying Careers – our Key Commitments

Around the campus of CU Denver, some of us like to joke that the Department of Communication should be called *the department of democracy*—for we see our mission as helping our students to work their ways into satisfying careers while also finding a calling, a passion, a project they can live with and grow with, all while contributing to the ethical, effective, and empowering debates that drive a healthy democracy. To help achieve these goals, we have structured our major around a number of key commitments, both intellectual and practical:

- To enable our students to practice community engagement, thus beginning their long careers as civically engaged citizens, we have partnered with Junior Achievement, a non-profit organization that has helped us to send 1,300 CU Denver students into the Denver Public Schools, where they have worked as teachers and mentors touching the lives of almost 16,000 pre-collegiate students. By tutoring and mentoring high school students, and by doing so within one of our introductory communication classes, we hope to cement the idea that education, democracy, and best communication practices go hand-in-hand. To supplement these lessons, we require all students to take an innovative course called "Communication, Social Justice, and Civic Engagement."

- To enable our students to enter the post-college marketplace with every possible advantage, we have built an internships program that includes partnerships with more than 75 local corporate and non-profit, media and arts, public relations, and civic groups. Our students work for a semester with the group of their choosing, thus gaining the valuable first-hand experiences and intellectual training that helps them land their dream jobs. In many cases, our students perform so well at their internship sites that they end up receiving job offers from their internship mentors.

- To enable our students to encounter the effects of globalization and the joys and perils of intercultural communication, we offer Denver-based classes on these topics as well as travel-study courses that journey to China, Guatemala, Italy, and Spain. Our students report that these travel study classes are mind-blowing and life-changing. Moreover, because we think education is one of the keys to advancing democracy in the developing world, we partner with the International College Beijing, where we have over 100 Chinese students working on their degree in communication.

- To enable our students to put their communication skills into action via student-led and faculty-supported campus groups, our faculty serve as advisors of and our students work as members of the National Association for the Advancement of Colored People, Amnesty International, the Buddhist Club, the International Culture Club, and others. In conjunction with these clubs, we support events such as the annual Mid-Autumn Festival (a big deal for our Chinese students) and recent panel discussions and film screenings about the death penalty and local initiatives to build alternatives to mass incarceration.

- To enable our students to make connections between communication, local politics, and civic engagement, we offer a number of classes wherein traditional classroom learning is merged with hands-on community experiences. In our "Health and Communities" class, for example, students study health communication while working with neighbors who need support navigating health issues. In our "Communication, Prisons, and Social Justice" class, students study the prison-industrial complex while also serving as tutors in a Denver area prison, working at local homeless shelters, and volunteering at other local organizations committed to ending the cycle of poverty, violence, and imprisonment. In our "Advanced Strategic Communication" course, students partner with local marketing and public relations firms for whom they help craft communication campaigns that embody effective and ethical messaging for the common good.

- To enable our students to begin learning how to practice best communication methods in mediated environments, we have launched a Department Facebook site, our Social Justice Project blog, and course-specific blogs, thus creating opportunities for written, recorded, and videoed communication (this is particularly helpful for our Chinese students, for whom these sites function as lifelines to the world of free speech). To make these mediated forms of communication into community-building activities, we recently hosted a "COMMunity" night of digital storytelling, where students and faculty were invited to show us their digital stories.

- To enable our students to think creatively about issues of gender and sexuality, race and ethnicity, and class and taste, we offer a range of courses such as "Communication and Diversity," "Communication and Gender," "Communication and Sexuality," and others, thus providing our students with structured opportunities for exploring some of the key issues driving political debates in the 21st century.

Unlimited Opportunities: Let your Imagination be your Guide

I could go on and on about the courses, events, or

programs we have launched to try to support the big ideas mentioned above, but will instead say simply that I think a degree in communication is invaluable because it offers students so many opportunities to take specific communication skills and ethics into any number of other career areas. With a degree in communication you can work for health care providers, international banks, various branches of government, community advocacy groups, any variety of media producers, advertising and marketing outfits, in both traditional and evolving forms of journalism, and hundreds of others.

If you let your imagination be your guide, rely upon your well-researched and elegantly argued communication to be your tools, and see civic engagement as a driving ethical commitment, then a degree in communication can be a wonderful first step toward building a successful career while following your calling.

Use your Communication Major as a Springboard into the World of Interdisciplinary Learning

It is important to remember, however, that no single degree or program can suffice to lead you on the exciting intellectual, civic, and career paths mentioned above—as a student of communication, then, you will need to learn from and work with fellow students and teachers from a wide array of units, centers, departments, and programs. Here at CU Denver, we accordingly encourage our students to think of themselves as interdisciplinary humanists.

Even as our students work toward their communication degree, we help them find fulfilling courses on our Anschutz Medical Campus, one of the fastest-growing medical campuses in North America; in the many other excellent departments within the College of Liberal Arts and Sciences; or with our "signature area" programs, which include minors in Women's and Gender Studies, Sustainability, Legal Studies, Ethnic Studies, Religious Studies, and Social Justice. Coupled with a robust School of Business, our College of Arts and Media (which runs its own record label, how cool is that?), and the School of Public Affairs—all wrapped up on an urban campus that sits in the very heart of Denver—CU Denver offers our students remarkable opportunities to craft fulfilling careers pegged to the local needs of our communities.

In summary, I hope to have persuaded you to consider communication as your major, and to use your major as a springboard into the world of interdisciplinary learning and civic engagement. If this sounds like a winning combination, if you like urban living, and especially if you would like to ski, hike, bike, Kayak, or rock climb in the Rocky Mountains, then the CU Denver Department of Communication is the perfect place to begin your journey.

COMMUNICATION FOR THE UNDECIDED STUDENTS, THEIR MAJOR &
CAREER ADVISORS, AND PARENTS: WHY STUDY COMMUNICATION?

Chapter 16: What is Communication, and Why Should You Study It? - Professor Gyromas Newman, PhD

Dr Gyromas W. Newman earned his Bachelor of Arts degree from the University of South Alabama with a double major in communication and philosophy and a minor in German. In the fall following his undergraduate graduation, Newman began pursuing his master of arts degree, also from the University of South Alabama, in Public and Corporate Communication. After completing of his masters, Newman started work on his Ph.D. in Communication and Information Sciences at the University of Alabama and attained his doctorate in May of 2012. Today, Newman is an assistant professor of communication at the University of Mobile.

'What Jobs can I Get with this Major?'

Communication as an academic discipline is essentially the study of how human beings create and share meaning. Visit a few different universities, and you'll soon realize that there are a number of different approaches to the study of communication. Some communication programs focus more on practical, field-specific applications, such as advertising, public relations, journalism, counseling, and so forth, whereas others focus more on a boarder, more holistic view of the communication process. Many universities, such as the University of Mobile, offer a mix of both applied and theoretical courses in communication. However, despite the broad scope of communication graduate and undergraduate programs, all programs in communication are united by the focus on the human process of creating and sharing meaning.

While in grade school, you may have heard someone say, "I just don't like math," to which a teacher replied, "But you use it every day whether or not you realize it." The teacher in this scenario probably went on to point out various ways the student used math in his or her daily life. Personally, I value math a great deal, and I realize that without it, our modern technological comforts would probably be nonexistent.

However, think, if you will, for a moment about what the world would be like without communication. What if we could not share meaning between ourselves? Not only would we not have our modern conveniences, we would not have society at all. The ability to share our ideas is an essential property of not only all of human progress but also what it means to be human in general. Although communication, at least at the basic level, comes naturally to us as humans, doing it well and truly understanding the communication process doesn't. That's why there is a major devoted to it.

When talking to students considering a major in communication, one of the first questions I usually hear is, 'What jobs can I get with this major?' I'll usually answer with the typical laundry list of jobs for communication majors such as journalist, public relations practitioner, ad designer, writer, counselor, and so on. However, I often follow that list by remarking that a communication major will help you with any job that requires you to articulate your own ideas and comprehend those of others.

In addition to preparing students to be marketable for a number of traditional jobs, communication majors are well prepared to take on and adapt to the jobs of the future. Technology and new media have opened up a wealth of new job opportunities and are reshaping existing jobs and business practices. Because the communication majors study not only the technical facts about a particular medium but also how that medium can be used most effectively to communicate a message, communication majors are generally ahead of the learning curve when it comes to new media. This makes communication majors marketable in a world dominated more and more by new media and technology.

In short, the job future looks bright for communication. An undergraduate or graduate degree in communication will remain marketable because it is centered on understanding and more effectively executing the process of creating and sharing meaning, which is essential to all human progress. A degree in communication will not only help students in the job market but also in their personal relationships because the skill of effective communication is essential to both.

The Benefits of Research

Research is essential to the success of any academic discipline, and communication is no exception. Many people hear the word research and think that it is only for professors, but in reality, a research degree in communication can be quite beneficial to students, even if they are not planning a career in academia. The most obvious benefit to a research degree is a thorough understanding of the theoretical underpinnings of the discipline. The study of research also teaches students to be better critical thinkers with the ability to systematically analyze problems. These skills are useful in any profession, not just academia.

Consulting is another area in which students can benefit from a research degree. Advertisers, public relations practitioners, network executives, and so on are always looking for new and innovative ways to reach their audiences and publics. Additionally, they want to know as much as they can about their audiences and publics, and all of this information comes from research. Some companies have in-house research teams to provide this information, and others contract independent researchers or research firms. Regardless, there are plenty of jobs in the field for a research degree that don't require working at a university.

Students are not the Only Ones Who can Benefit from Research

Communication practitioners can gain valuable insight into the workings of a number of phenomena relevant to their applied fields of communication from reading research studies. In other words, consulting communication research can help communication practitioners do their jobs more effectively. Arguably, the reason more communication practitioners don't take advantage of published research in the field is because they don't know about it or don't have access to it.

Online databases house thousands of journal publications in communication, but access to these databases is usually granted only to universities or similar organizations that have purchased pricey subscriptions. Such subscriptions make this information highly accessible to professors and students but not to the general public.

For the public, access to one journal article stored online can cost $32.00 (U.S.) or more. Although there are more cost effective ways for the public to access journal articles such as through a local library, the initial price quote yielded by a quick Google search may deter many would-be readers from searching any further. In short, if researchers want more communication practitioners to take advantage of their work, the academic community needs to come up with ways of making research more accessible to those outside of academia.

Closing Thoughts

In closing, a lot of us go through life never realizing how the basic things we do everyday shape our conception of our past, our present, and our future; however, there are few things that have the potential to shape so much of our public and private lives the way communication does. The way we interact with people, the messages we receive, the messages we send, how we process information, and the meaning we create and share determines how we understand our past, how we make sense of our present, and influences the direction of our future. It is communication which both connects and divides us as people. Because communication has such an impact on all of our lives, I counter the question "Why should I study communication?" with "Why shouldn't I?" To date, I've yet to think of a good reason.

Chapter 17: Why Study Communication? Professor Lisa Cuklanz, PhD

Dr Lisa M. Cuklanz is Professor and Chair of the Communication department. Her central research interest is in critical examinations of mass media representations of gendered violence. Dr. Cuklanz is the former director of Women's Studies at Boston College and past co-chair of the Radcliffe Graduate Consortium in Women's Studies. She has served as Visiting Fulbright Professor of Communication Studies at Hong Kong Baptist University, and as Harvard Law School Fellow in Law and Communication. She is author of two books published by the University of Pennsylvania Press, co-editor (with Sujata Moorti) of a collection on global media representations of gendered violence, as well as numerous articles published in journals including Critical Studies in Media Communication, Communication Quarterly, Journal of Gender Studies, Women's Studies in Communication, and Communication Studies. Prof. Cuklanz's website can be found at https://www2.bc.edu/~cuklanz/

Communication Coursework and Internship Opportunities

The field of Communication Studies is extremely broad in the United States, and can vary widely from one school to the other in terms of what subjects are included or excluded, what courses are offered, and what career aspirations are common among students. Some departments of Communication offer courses in theater and dance, telecommunications, journalism, or advertising, but our curriculum at Boston College does not include these subject areas. The Communication Department at Boston College offers courses in three subject areas: media and cultural studies, rhetoric, and interpersonal communication. Because our department is situated within the School of Arts and Sciences, our curriculum focuses on the more academic side of communication including research methods, theory, and critical thinking rather than on applications students consider more hands-on pre-professional training.

However, along with our coursework we offer two options for internships in relevant industries, and a majority of our students take advantage of these opportunities. A large percentage of our students also choose to study abroad for one semester, and some even go abroad for the whole junior year.

While many of our students go on to graduate school in fields represented within the department, others choose to pursue a graduate degree in related fields such as journalism, law, and business. A particularly important part of our curriculum is the requirement that students take two writing intensive seminars. In these upper-level courses, students are required to write a 25-page research paper. In this way, students are quite comfortable with research and writing by the time they complete the major.

Why the Communication Major is so Popular?

The Communication major has been one of the three most popular majors at Boston College for over a decade, and we have approximately 1,000 majors at graduation time each Spring. There are probably several things that make the major so popular among undergraduate students.

First, it offers an excellent balance of intellectually rigorous coursework with a sense of purpose in terms the potential of a fulfilling future career in a related industry. Our students are able to find internship placements in communication industries including broadcasting (television and radio), print media (newspapers and magazines), online communication (social media and online publications), advertising, public relations and film, as well as in the advertising and public relations side of many other industries including higher education, law, sports, and event planning. Our recent graduates work for ESPN, Google, Youtube, and many other popular and cutting edge companies in communication industries.

By developing their academic skills, such as public speaking, critical thinking, and message analysis fully through our research-based curriculum, students prepare themselves to be independent thinkers and decision makers in a wide range of fields. I think students also really enjoy the communication major because many of our courses examine industries, texts, and phenomena that are part of our everyday experience. A frequent comment on student course evaluations is that the student found one of our courses relevant to their life in the real world. In courses on Communication Criticism, Media Violence, Persuasion, or Interpersonal Communication, students are learning about experiences and texts that they will encounter and think about on a regular basis.

Students choose our major because our courses offer a depth of understanding, insight, and analysis that students use as a part of their interaction with the world during and after college.

Our major is both relevant and exciting for students, and it helps prepare them for a wide range of careers in a broad set up industries, without getting overly focused on practical details such as specific software, equipment or practices that will have a very short shelf life. Our students are smart, highly engaged, and ambitious.

Higher education in the US is often known for its emphasis on original thinking, classroom participation, and seminar-style learning environments in which the classroom format is more like a conversation than a lecture.

Summer Study Abroad and Other Programs

Although we have some introductory courses that are more lecture-based, most of our courses have small class sizes and run on the seminar format in which the professor engages with students in a focused conversation based on a series of questions. In this way, students take an active part in the learning process and have an opportunity to demonstrate their preparation, general knowledge, and capacity for original thinking. The best student comments are those that draw from the material under discussion and make connections to previous course materials, other courses, or insights related to the world outside the classroom.

Boston College offers a large number of programs in which students can engage with the world and learn more about themselves through service and/or introspection. In addition to service trips in the US and abroad, BC offers weekend retreats, undergraduate research opportunities and grants, mentoring programs, and department-based summer study abroad programs in which faculty members take groups of students from their own departments abroad to undertake a focused study of some aspect of a different culture.

Our students take part in all of these programs, and the department has recently offered a summer course on Popular Culture in France, taught in Bordeaux. In our department, faculty members and students are encouraged and expected to develop collegial relationships that will facilitate both learning and engagement in the learning process on the part of students.

Research and Publications

Faculty members at Boston College are pursuing a wide range of interesting research projects and have published over three dozen books. Faculty research interests in many ways reflect what students like best about majoring in Communication. Most of us study aspects of contemporary popular culture, global media, ideological functions of mainstream discourses, or patterns of interpersonal or public communication. The connections to some processes and content that we face every day outside of the university context make the work inherently interesting. A list of books published by our faculty members since 2007 can be found on the department website at http://www.bc.edu/content/bc/schools/cas/comm unication/publications/books.html.

Our most recent faculty book is a collection of essays about the television program Saturday Night Live co-edited by Dr. Matt Siekiewicz (Title: Saturday Night Live and American TV). One of our faculty members, Dr. Marilyn Matelski, has published 14 books. Among her many publishers is Common Ground Press, and Australian University Press. Dr. Michael Keith has authored or edited more than 20 books and is has most recently published several works of fiction. His most successful book to date is a textbook entitled The Radio Station, now in its 8th edition.

My work focuses on media representations of gendered violence, and I have published three books and many articles in this general area, with two more books coming out shortly. My 2006 article co-authored with Sujata Moorti examines linkages between gender, crime, and parenthood in the prime television drama Law and Order: Special Victims Unit, a series that is in its 15th season this year. The article examines the ways in which female criminality is linked both with motherhood and with severe and lasting trauma to children. The full text is available at http://www.tandfonline.com/doi/full/10.1080/07 393180600933121#.UqtVKI11F XY.

Our faculty also publishes in a range of journals within the field of Communication as well as outside the immediate field. In fact, most faculty members in our department have some link to interdisciplinary work with other departments, universities, or even in other countries. Professor Fishman studies crisis communication in a wide range of contexts, Professor Sienkiewicz is an expert in Middle Eastern media, and Professor Matelski travels and writes about many countries including China and Cuba. Our faculty work and publish with colleagues in the fields of law, medicine, Jewish studies, women's studies, American studies, African and African Diaspora Studies, international studies, psychology, sociology, history, and political science. A list of journal articles published by our faculty since 2000 can be found at http://www.bc.edu/content/bc/schools/cas/comm unication/publications/articles. html.

The field of Communication is relatively young in the United States, and many of the oldest universities and colleges to do not have Communication departments. The schools that offer Communication have found it to be extremely popular among students, and Boston College is certainly no exception. The combination of critical thinking, theoretical frameworks, practical knowledge, and relevance to the world outside of the classroom all combine to make the major one of the most popular on campus. The increasing salience of communication processes, texts, technologies, and industries to our everyday functioning as individuals and as a society will likely mean that the field of Communication continues to expand and gain in popularity.

Chapter 18: Why Study Public Relations and Social Media? – Abby Dress, APR

Abby Dress, whose career has spanned high-tech, medical devices, health care, the environment and the arts, is an associate professor of media arts at LIU Post, where she has directed its public relations degree program since 1993. She balances academia with professional work as the founder of Smith & Dress, a marketing communications firm, serving clients including Yellowstone National Park, Precipart, Canon and American Heart Association. Her campaigns were recognized nationally with a 2006 Clarion Award by the Association of Women in Communication, reprinted in the Graphic Design USA Annual Award issues, honored by the Biomedical Marketing Association and described in the book, "Publicity for Non-profits." Professor Dress is an accredited member of the Public Relations Society of America, judges the Silver Anvil and Big Apple Awards and advises a student PRSSA chapter at LIU Post. She also is a member of the American Institute of Graphic Arts, New York Women in Communications, National Association of Women Business Owners and Media Ecology Association. She capped her B.A. in fine arts with an M.B.A. and is working on a Ph.D. at New York University.

So you Want to Study Public Relations? What's That?

Content and communication are top priorities today, not just in America. As adoption of a digital lifestyle has become more pervasive, you should know that the field of public relations has burgeoned significantly with options for lots of portals for you to create content and communication. That means there are lots of opportunities for careers globally in government agencies, businesses large and small, non-governmental organizations or nonprofits and membership associations that serve these groups or individuals who work in them. Additionally, there are an abundance of agencies of various types and sizes that provide services to support an organization's needs or fulfill these communication efforts. In any case, the field of public relations has moved beyond its publicity role to include and manage much more.

Growing in Reputation and Importance

Public relations practitioners continue to reinvent

their influence and impact as their efforts continue to gain momentum in the 21st century. This has moved a long way from the stunts of P.T. Barnum to promote his circus during the late 1800s in the United States when publicity men flourished. Ultimately these activities gave way to the public relations counsel envisioned by 20th century legend Edward Bernays as America modernized and grew in its world stature throughout the 1900s. Practitioners assisted marketers with special events, launched new products and services, increased brand recognition, and helped diffuse negative sentiment during a crisis. They influenced citizens through voting initiatives, swayed public opinion through advocacy campaigns about issues, and represented important figures in the public eye.

In some ways, there were two triggers that really focused attention on the value of public relations in the last quarter of the 20th century. As daily newspapers became financially stressed under competitive pressure for their readers and advertising revenues from broadcast and cable media, family-owned businesses like the Chandlers in Los Angeles, Medill Patterson in Chicago, and Ochs-Sulzbergers in New York sold out or merged to create mega-businesses known as media conglomerates. Deregulation or relaxed rules of ownership by the Federal Communications Commission and the U.S. Congress in 1981, created new media tycoons, such as Ted Turner, John C. Malone, Rupert Murdoch, and Sumner Redstone, who scooped up available media from movies and cable stations to radio and television to build their holdings, too. This concentrated power and controlled dissemination of content in fewer hands. This also meant fewer jobs for reporters and editors. All of a sudden a writer for the Wall Street Journal appeared on television, and then a TV newscaster was heard on radio. Journalists not only could work across various media, but also this became a requisite part of their jobs.

While this was a beneficial time for journalists already in the business to expand their roles, it also meant reduced numbers of job openings for new journalism graduates in the U.S. The universities and colleges offering journalism degrees added courses or developed whole programs in public relations. How could journalism programs survive when the job market kept contracting? Many college programs adopted public relations coursework not only to study the relevant theories of communication, but also to take advantage of the new opportunities that were simultaneously on the rise as America embraced public relations

However, a good number of these original courses

were taught by journalism professors. What journalists and public relations practitioners had in common was they could write well, and they knew what the media wanted. Indeed there was some crossover in the job market between the two fields. Though many journalism professors did not possess the focus, objectives or tactical knowledge of the public relations business professional that had evolved into the business practice at the time, this period gave rise to formalized programs in public relations education.

The recession of 1987 finally positioned public relations in the business world. Suddenly cash poor, due to crashing stock prices, companies cut their advertising and marketing expenditures and, in some cases, eliminated them all together. They deployed public relations tactics to garner stories in the media to keep their brand messages alive and used more events and activities to reach citizens and consumers directly. Organizations without corporate communication departments or individuals established and hired them to manage and implement public relations programs. In addition to serving the marketing efforts with product or service publicity, public relations practitioners became part of or headed up corporate communications departments, which reported into the chief executive officer suite.

Opportunities in Public Relations

This has been a growing trend since: fewer journalism positions and increased public relations opportunities with expanding responsibilities. From early web content and branded messages to employee communications and special events, public relations has grown in stature and specialty. In fact, the field is somewhat confusing because there are so many sub-disciplines known by different names today. Regardless of administrative titles, practitioners work in diverse areas, such as product or service publicity, as press agents, special events, investor relations, governmental relations, community relations, social responsibility, lobbying, development, and public affairs, etc. They use today's media platforms as well as develop and implement direct strategies to inform or influence audiences.

Since citizens and consumers whatever age can access information from a variety of sources today, the way they make decisions likewise has fundamentally changed. In particular, the way organizations prepare and produce this information also seems to be changing with public relations continuing to extend its role. Still not licensed as Bernays espoused, practitioners of public relations in this century now enjoy challenging leadership roles as they report into the presidents of companies and organizations of different sizes whether they are public entities or major multinational enterprises. They communicate through various media platforms, oversee relationships internally, and often bypass media to reach out directly to constituent audiences regardless of their numbers or location. In some cases, they even direct the branding programs to develop key messages and to jumpstart the aligned digital marketing, advertising, public relations, and social media initiatives.

At the same time, public relations has become a discipline in demand by business and other organizations. Public relations is closer to the perspectives, objectives and concerns of corporate CEOs than any other communication or marketing discipline says the Public Relations Society of America ("PR by the Numbers"). It not only sees the whole corporate picture, but also drives the business outcomes for organizational success.

Yet, unlike management, marketing, finance or operations business concentrations, the public relations major rarely is offered in business schools–where only a course or two perhaps is available on the undergraduate level. This major in the U.S. developed for the most part in schools of journalism or the newer communication schools that developed during the peak of media concentration. This means young high school students, who become knowledgeable about the range of opportunities in public relations and interested in business, may find alternative, enjoyable career paths in this discipline. Like most fields, personal networks in addition to excellent skills help the process along.

Moreover, the field of public relations affords individuals lots of choices for full-time, part-time, freelance and entrepreneurial work. As a result, this has been a bonus to young females, particularly when they start families of their own. In fact, the field is an ideal career path for women, who have become vice presidents, directors, partners or owners of their own businesses. Likewise it can be attractive to minorities. Minority- and women-owned firms continue to emerge and thrive. They are entrenched in serving their communities and assisting local and major campaigns communicate to their specialized audiences even in their own languages.

Where Public Relations Students Fit

Public relations is about information or messages

and where or how to communicate to audiences. Large service-based communication conglomerates now control major global holdings, which means they own advertising agencies, public relations firms, web design entities and digital solution providers. It appears that some multi-tiered national and global campaigns now use the public relations firms to manage the process when their contracted sister groups are involved. Integrated marketing or integrated communication finally seems to have arrived. The public relations firm develops the messaging and strategies, while the ad agency may buy traditional advertising, and the digital web firm may purchase the sponsored ads and other digital real estate. The social media programs now are tied into the larger public relations firms. They "borrow" the look to mirror the advertising and brand the social platforms similarly.

College students schooled in the broad public relations function, though, can find employment experience in any of these individual entities for internships, part-time jobs or permanent ones when they graduate. They can use their writing, technology (business, graphic, or social), management and planning abilities, research and analysis skills, and their team-based experience to obtain first-tier positions, which may not be called public relations per se. Depending on their interest and abilities, they can move up the ladders in these specialty areas or move on to broader-based responsibilities.

With a solid grounding in public relations education on the undergraduate level, young professionals in the U.S. really do not need a graduate degree, since experience–including internships–counts heavily. Only when their corporation or organization requires a degree for advancement will a graduate degree become necessary. Also, the coursework in graduate degrees resonates better when individuals have some real-life business experience first. Since the field keeps advancing and changing, young professionals should remain current with new technologies, the metrics for evaluation, and more. By joining a professional society or association, young practitioners can take advantage of workshops and webinars as well as build their networks of colleagues. This is one of the advantages when students attend undergraduate programs that feature Public Relations Student Society of America or PRSSA chapters: they can leverage their student memberships after graduation into professional ones.

Multiple language ability is a plus in the field. Many international students have flocked to

American universities and colleges with comprehensive public relations degree programs. They speak English and come to America to learn the business of public relations, increase their written skills, become adept in the planning process, apply technologies to content, communicate effectively, and monitor the results for effectiveness or required change. Then again, these international students often speak and write two, three or four languages. When they return to their home countries to look for jobs, they can position themselves as knowledgeable and flexible employees for global assignments and advancement. To remain competitive, more U.S. students must become fluent in a second language to take advantage of the communication opportunities within multi-national organizations.

How Social Media Fares

Though social media is the new rage today as an outgrowth of the internet capability, so were radio and television in their own times. Social media's mobility, on the other hand, affords 24/7 accessibility for audience connection however broadly or narrowly defined. When organizations first used social media, their communication programs were standalone programs. But, as they were explored and more individuals became social savvy, social media quickly became embedded into the overall communication strategies and an integral part of campaigns. Additionally, because of their immediacy, they enjoy wide use, but they also pose communication threats. As such, new specialties have quickly emerged to deploy their advantages and reduce their downsides. This means job opportunities abound in social media.

From advocacy positions, likes, tweets, review blogs or brand sharing sites, social media have become accepted tools of or platforms for communication. Their managers tend to be younger, but they are disciplined, skilled practitioners. Good writing, even in "social speak," must be correct, timely, and appropriate. Use of metrics for evaluation measurement is key to effective social media programs. How social media should be integrated into mainstream communication programs, what are appropriate objectives, how to convince individuals they should visit a site or like or retweet something are the vital elements studied by majors. Just because many people use mobile media, does not mean they can manage it. Young folks certainly are immersed in social media technology, but they must learn more about the business of social media. Seasoned practitioners now use social media expertly, value its possibilities and hire young graduates with excellent skills.

Socially Correct to Audiences Directly

The biggest change in this digital world is that public relations initiatives can talk directly to consumers, customers and other audiences via social media –Twitter, Facebook, email, texts, websites and more. Today, organizations can push their messages through to their respective consumers of information and bypass journalists. This also has broad implications.

Already, the Pew Research Center's Project for Excellence in Journalism in its Annual Report on American Journalism 2013 ("State of the News Media 2013") indicated that news reporting resources have converged with online opportunities to take their messages directly to the audiences, too. News outlet sites also have lost advertising revenues as social media sites have been commodified to increase theirs. At the same time, most Americans today, according to Pew, receive their news from friends or family, whether via social media or actual word of mouth ("State of the News Media 2013"). Lost revenue for legacy media combined with the diminishing interest in news by many individuals is on the increase.

Additionally, there is evidence that news sources

recycle so much information that there is a lack of original news, according to a three-decade study in Philadelphia reported in 2006 by the Project for Excellence in Journalism, says media reform advocates Bob McChesney and John Nichols in "The Death and Life of American Journalism: The Media Revolution that Will Begin the World Again." The new native advertising, much like the advertorial, is purchased space written by public relations pros to look like editorial copy. Muddled messages can be confusing. Implications for misinformation and disinformation will proliferate without authoritative sources for news. It also means consumers of this information must be highly literate to sort through information whether recirculated or not. Commodification of news along with the absence of coverage is dangerous precedent that can affect whether an informed citizenry develops or not.

The speed of communication and the fact it is direct to audiences has implications on many fronts for the receivers of this information. Since these social media companies have grown and become public companies, like Facebook and Google, they must become profitable entities. As such, they collect and mine preferences of and information about their users. This compiled data is used to attract advertisers interested in targeting specific audiences. Advertising generates revenue streams for social media. Media literacy now is more important than ever so that citizens and consumers can discern authentic messages, authentic senders, and what is truthful and relevant.

As a result of these important changes taking place in media, university faculties are looking at many of these issues. They compare metrics of the media platforms, conduct surveys, or initiate focus groups to determine perspectives or preferences of users. They are interested in what users think, how they use social media, and the negative/positive effects. They look at the ethical practices, too. A number of professors have advanced the idea that social media is addictive and that citizens and consumers are consumed by this flood of information that is pushed to them.

Other professors of media advocate taking a digital fast from any and all digital devices and media–cell phones, tablets, computers, televisions, music, movies, and more. Using their classrooms as laboratories, professors and students record their feelings as they refrain from using media. Other academics are conducting formalized studies and involving students in their process. In the U.S., the PRSA in periodic reports with the Association for Education in Journalism and Mass Communication has advocated for years that a research class should be one of the five to seven courses programs that run as part of public relations concentrations.

As research has proliferated in universities and monitoring organizations, practitioners likewise are looking at market intelligence and identifying audience behaviors and reception in order to run their programs more effectively. They hire internal researchers and outside research firms to collect data and interpret findings. There is an emphasis on upfront research to design the program and again when it ends to assess the outcomes. In the U.S., the PRSA continues to promote research and measurement. The society not only offers workshops and webinars to increase its use, but also it sets the standards for the field.

Public Relations Programs to Consider

The practice of public relations is more than media connections today. It is about information and building relationships with audiences. From online communities and real hometowns to local efforts and global campaigns, communication programs across multiple media platforms can involve young thinkers right from the get go – especially when they bring excellent skills to the table.

That means you. If you are interested in public relations or communications, then build your skills though a major or minor. The more you know about the field and the more skills you can offer, the more you can bring to an internship and employer today. Writing is an essential business skill required by most organizations, but not necessarily emphasized in business program coursework. Look for programs that provide comprehensive courses as a foundation and then expand on the learning through case examination, research, business and marketing classes, as well as the graphics side including video. Digital and social media coursework also give you an edge into the marketplace, too. Test the waters through internships to see what you like and what you are good at. There are lots of options and career paths that let you explore and grow.

Reference List and Suggested References

"About the PRSA: Advancing the Profession and the   Professional." http://www.prsa.org/AboutPRSA/#.U6cb3hZbTwI . Retrieved June 20, 2014.

"Five Reasons People Don't Think Social Media is a Real Job." PR Daily. April 12, 2013. http://www.prdaily.com/Main/Articles/14255.asp x# Retrieved April 14, 2013.

McChesney, Robert and John Nichols. "The Death
and Life of American Journalism: The Media
Revolution that Will Begin the World Again." New
York: Nation Books, 2010. 36. Print

"Media and Communications." Occupational
Handbook. United States Department of Labor.
http://www.bls.gov/ooh/media-and-
communication/home.htm. Retrieved June 15,
2014.

"PR by the Numbers." PRSA Newsroom. Public
Relations Society of America website.
http://media.prsa.org/pr-by-the-number/
Retrieved June 1. 2014.

"State of the News Media 2013." Pew Research
Journalism Project.
http://stateofthemedia.org/2013/overview-5/.
Retrieved November 22, 2013.

"State of the News Media 2014." Pew Research
Journalism Project.
http://www.journalism.org/packages/state-of-the-
news-media-2014/ Retrieved May 16, 2014.

Sullivan, John. 1 May 2011. "PR Industry Fills
Vacuum Left by Shrinking Newsrooms." Pro
Publica website.
http://www.propublica.org/article/pr-industry-

fills-vacuum-left-by-shrinking-newsrooms/single.
Retrieved May 22, 2014.

"The Internet of Things will Thrive by 2025." Pew
Research   Internet   Project.
http://www.pewinternet.org. Retrieved May 16,
2014.

Weiner, Mark. "How Proctor & Gamble Made the
PR-to-Sales   Connection."   Excerpted   from
Unleashing the Power of Public Relations: A
Contrarian's   Guide   to   Marketing   and
Communication. CW   Bulletin.   International
Association of Business Communicators website.
http://www.iabc.com/cwb/archive/2006/0906/po
werofPR.htm. Retrieved June 20, 2014.

Worldometers: Real   Time   World   Statistics.
http://www.worldometers.info. Retrieved May 14,
2014.

Wynne, Robert. 4 September 2013. "Public
Relations, Explained." Forbes website.
http://www.forbes.com/sites/robertwynne/2013/0
9/04/public-relations-explained// Retrieved May
22, 2014.

Chapter 19 - Multiplatform Journalism: Purposes and Prospects – Professor Mike Dillon, PhD

Dr. Mike Dillon is Chair of the Department of Journalism and Multimedia Arts at Duquesne University in Pittsburgh. Dr Dillon teaches in the areas of Print Journalism and Mass Media. He has authored or co-authored two books and numerous scholarly articles and book chapters. Prior to his academic career, Dillon was a newspaper reporter and won 15 awards for journalistic excellence in five separate reporting and writing categories. From 2000-2003, he was Associate Editor and Chief Writer of Primo Magazine, a national glossy. Dillon has profiled author Norman Mailer, pop legend Tony Bennett, and iconic football star Johnny Unitas. He continues to freelance and his essays have appeared in New York Newsday, the San Francisco Chronicle, the Pittsburgh Post-Gazette and the Dallas Morning News. He's is the recipient of a university Presidential Scholarship Award and a Creative Teaching Award. He has a long-standing relationship with the September 11th Families Association and directs an internship program that each summer sends two JMA

*students to work at "Tribute," a museum and
visitor center on the rim of Ground Zero.*

Choosing Journalism as a Major: Role, Function, Knowledge, Skills

Journalism represents a system of civic inquiry into the forces and conditions that shape our lives. The investigative aspect of journalism teaches tenacity in inquiry and rigor in analysis. Journalists also work within moral frameworks and find guidance in the ethical codes of The Society of Professional Journalists, the American Society of News Editors and other professional groups.

Some journalists are specialists in a particular subject area, such as economics, technology or the environment, and some are generalists who have the knowledge base and intellectual agility to cover a wide range of subjects. In either case, journalists must sift through vast amounts of data, often controlled by agencies that do not want them to have it, weigh conflicting accounts from self-interested parties, draw connections between different kinds of information and then interpret and shape a narrative that is accurate, comprehensive and precise, and yet accessible to diverse publics who are awash in a sea of competing narratives – and they must do all this on deadline.

Delivery is another key facet of journalism. Traditionally, journalists created accounts of the world that publics sought out; today, journalists must find audiences in the mobilesphere and then adapt stories to the platform most likely to engage them – the equivalent of hitting multiple moving targets simultaneously.

And so the student of journalism is a student of humanity and of the systems that publics, cultures, corporations and governments create to organize themselves, impose order and share meaning. A journalist is a synthesizer whose ability to discover, identify significance and provide context for events and information has obvious value in a wide variety of career fields beyond journalism.

Today's journalist is also a technological innovator who engages multiple publics across a variety of platforms, each with its own texture and grammars. This versatility across the realms of inquiry, narrative construction and delivery positions a person trained in the methods of journalism as a valued researcher and communicator in fields as diverse as multimedia production, sports media, law, marketing, and government service. Duquesne University Journalism graduates are working in all of these fields – and also as journalists, of course.

A logical question arises: Why should a student major in journalism to master this knowledge and these skills if he or she might choose to work in a field outside of journalism? The answer is simple: No other major teaches this distinct blend of skills, knowledge and communicative proficiency. Journalism provides a foundation in research, story conception, storytelling and production that is not to be found elsewhere in the American curriculum. And it does so in a context that emphasizes the importance of civic engagement and social responsibility.

The Duquesne University Journalism and Multimedia Arts curriculum employs a "Swiss army knife" approach to pedagogy. That means that in addition to learning media theory, our students are expected to develop proficiency in at least two areas of multimedia production (for instance, writing and photography) and competencies in several other areas (such as database management/data scraping, visual design, videography, and broadcast studio production). Our rationale for adopting this model, which has proven successful, is that if students cannot immediately find employment in their area of proficiency, they are qualified for jobs for which they possess competencies. In many cases, those "competency" jobs allow graduates to find initial employment with firms that later have openings in the area in which the graduate is proficient and most wants to work.

The Uses of Journalism Research

Increasingly, U.S. graduate programs are stressing broad-based "media studies" programs rather than focusing on particular media industries such as journalism or public relations. The lines are blurring between journalism, entertainment, public relations, advertising and even foundation initiatives. "Sponsored content" blends marketing with news. New foundations like ProPublica, the Pulitzer Center and the Center for Public Integrity (a 2014 Pulitzer Prize winner) practice the kind of investigative reporting traditional news organizations specialized in before their revenues – and therefore resources – declined. Those organizations – including broadcast networks, National Public Radio and the *Washington Post*, to name just a few – are now paying clients of foundations like CPI and ProPublica.[xviii]

And so there is fertile ground for graduate study and research into journalism and related cultural industries. The Journalism and Multimedia Arts Department at Duquesne recently concluded a $127,000 research grant from the Knight Foundation to study the differences in perceived credibility of video news shot with traditional gear as opposed to mobile gear, including tablets and smart phones. That study will seed several journal articles and the grant report itself is available to professionals and academics at our departmental website.[xix]

The Journalism and Multimedia Arts department offers M.S. programs in Media Management, Web Design and Development, and Multimedia. Our typical student is a recent graduate or early-career professional who seeks additional education and training in order to qualify for advancement: for instance, an assignment editor or on-air reporter at a broadcast affiliate might take our Media Management curriculum as a step towards moving into station management.[xx]

Academic Research and Journalism Practice

Practitioners are highly interested in applied academic research; less so in theoretical research. The Duquesne/Knight Foundation study has been the subject of inquiries from several news organizations that are navigating the complex transition from traditional modes of content/delivery/revenue to a mobile world where each citizen-consumer's news stream represents a diverse blend of sources instead of one or two "branded" news products such as the Pittsburgh *Post-Gazette* or the *New York Times*.

In addition, Dr. William Gibbs of the JMA Department has conducted human-computer interaction studies that track and analyze how people navigate Web sites and applied his findings in partnership with the *Post-Gazette* to help redesign part of the online newspaper's Web site. It seems likely that applied academic research will continue to attract the interest and funding of news organizations and foundations trying to adapt to fast-shifting mobile environments.

Media Ethics *is* one area of theory that generates interest among practitioners, educators, civic leaders, students and citizens. Mobile devices do more than just provide instant access to news, entertainment, gossip, and social networks – they serve as megaphones for anyone who wants to join the digital conversation, which is often rife with misinformation, disinformation, sensation and even cruelty – notably in the case of internet "trolls" who often post uncivil and mean-spirited comments on stories produced by legitimate news sites.

Practitioners, their subjects, and their interactive audiences have largely been left to navigate the chaotic online landscape without a moral roadmap or a sense of how new dynamics that shape public discourse might be moored to ethical principles that have served journalists –as well as the larger public forum – through previous eras of upheaval and rapid technological change.

According to the Pew Research Center, in 2012 half of Americans got their news from a digital source rather than a print, broadcast or cable outlet – a substantial increase from just two years earlier. More than a one-fifth of survey respondents reported receiving news from social media sites.[xxi] But they are not simply receiving digitally what they once received in print. Digital content and delivery raises new problems in ethics, particularly in the areas of privacy, piracy and the anonymous nature of much online participation.

As deeply held practices and assumptions about journalism have vanished or been transformed, the relevance of enduring ethical assumptions and principles that served to regulate our democratic marketplace of ideas have been problematized. Just as newspapers discovered in the 1990s that attempting to shoehorn their print templates into the online universe was a recipe for civic irrelevance and economic disaster, so journalists and citizens today are discovering that the moral rulebook that emerged from the age of print is ill-suited to the world of new media. Do Aristotle, Kant, Mill and other touchstones of ethical philosophy really have anything relevant to say about Twitter and Buzzfeed? How do journalists adapt enduring ethical and civic values to respond to unprecedented forms of communication? Media Ethics represents a fertile area of theoretical research with tremendous practical value.[xxii]

Best Practices: The Multiplatform Approach

I believe the future of media education in general, and journalism education in particular, lies with a multiplatform approach that facilitates convergence and encourages adaptability in a world of fast-changing technologies, platforms and revenue models.

Multiplatform media education focuses on the creation of layers of meaning.
Multiplatform messages are rooted in: ideas and the skillful written expression of those ideas; sound and audio; still and moving images; and graphics, which in post-production are blended into a totality that is ideally suited to reach the platform(s) it is designed to reach.

Layers of mediation are both conceptual and tool-based. While students learn to use tools to create a vast array of media messages, the conceptual layers that underlie message creation must drive curriculum. Messages are expressions of ideas. Without an idea, a slickly produced message is an empty vessel. So at a conceptual level students have to understand what they are trying to say, why they are trying to say it, who they are trying to say it to, the special qualities of the tools and platforms they are using to say it, what effects and feedback they might anticipate, and how their message might contribute to a larger cultural conversation that is constantly in the process of transformation. These are timeless considerations that would be familiar to Socrates, Jesus, Locke, Jefferson, Stanton, Du Bois, and King – any thoughtful person wishing to reach the consciousness of his or her fellow beings.

The conceptual layer of media education is foremost for two additional reasons:

Tools change. If students learn only to adeptly manipulate tools in a particular moment – and in some American journalism programs, they do – they will be at sea when the tools inevitably change. The Duquesne University Journalism program values an ethos of adaptability and compels students to understand the conceptual basis of mediated communication so they are able to embrace changes in tools as new opportunities arise to express those concepts more effectively.

Our students are clearly focused on pursuing careers in the fields of Journalism, Public Relations, Advertising, Multimedia, Web Development and Sports Media. Their work will have a huge impact on the content, tone and tenor of cultural conversation because over the course of their careers, the messages they create will reach millions and millions of people. That is power that can be used responsibly or irresponsibly. We teach our students to be ethical, responsible and mindful in employing the power of mediated communication.

Duquesne University students won't simply "one day" produce mediated communication in their communities; they are *already* doing so through student media, internships and a curriculum that takes full advantage of Pittsburgh's urban setting. Public Relations and Advertising classes work with real clients. The Magazine Journalism class produces an in-print and online interactive magazine called *Off the Bluff*, which focuses on Pittsburgh's neighborhoods.[xxiii] The Investigative Journalism class conducted and published an online multimedia chronicle of the economic decline and future prospects of a typical Mon Valley steel town.[xxiv] The Web Design course helped redesign an online section of a major metropolitan newspaper and our journalism students are reporting, editing and delivering news using mobile devices.

Mainstream journalism is currently experiencing a crisis, as audience members themselves now produce news content and relay it – typically without charge or compensation – on Twitter and other social media platforms. Until a stable and workable revenue model for online news is created, news organizations will struggle to profit from the high-quality content they produce. In addition, traditional news organizations cannot match the pace at which regular citizens with smart phones tweet information and images about events they witness.

Even as mainstream news outlets continue to experience disruption, however, the role of journalism will retain value as "a credibility filter that sifts through all this data and highlights what is worth reading, understanding and trusting."[xxv] Alas, the quality of "amateur information" has not matched the massive quantity of data now available to consumers, which means that independent voices with journalistic training can stand out and attract audiences – and thus revenue – for blogs, e-newsletters, and specialized niche reporting. Not everyone who succeeds in journalism will do so because they work for a brand-name news organization.

Forward-thinking programs predicate their curriculum on the idea that tomorrow's journalists will operate in a radically new media environment and they reject the prevailing attitude among so-called legacy news organizations since the dawn of the Internet in the early 1990s that success hinges on translating traditional functions and approaches into "new media " platforms – an old-wine-in-a-new-bottle approach.

In fact, "digital savvy" journalism educators are doing a better job of pointing the way forward than journalism professionals, who continue to resist multimedia storytelling skills, according to a 2014 Poynter survey. "It appears that educators have listened to the debate about the need to change, at least enough to acknowledge the importance of new skills."[xxvi]

ProPublica Editor and former Wall Street Journal managing editor Paul Steiger urges journalists to be open-minded and not reflexively dismiss digital news organizations that blend journalism with entertainment or even contests and trivia (both staples of the 19th Century New Journalism that represented the zenith of influence and profitability for newspapers). He singled out BuzzFeed as an alluring new platform for news despite its many non-news features. "It's time that we embrace the dominance of the web, not just say 'Digital First,' but mean it. News platforms are rising frequently on the Internet; some, like BuzzFeed, are amassing huge traffic and edging toward profitability. If I were the young journalists and journalism students here, that's the kind of team I'd want to join."[xxvii]

Similarly, in his influential *Journalism Next*, Mark Briggs urges journalists and news executives to accept the fact that the mobileverse operates by fundamentally different principles than traditional print and video. "To survive and thrive in the digital age ... journalists must adopt a new way of thinking and approaching their craft. Learning the skills and technology is actually the easy part. Recognizing you are part of a new information ecosystem, aka 'the future,' is the steeper hill to climb."[xxviii]

A recent Pew Foundation report provides some key insights into the composition of that ecosystem:

"At a time when print newsrooms continue to shed jobs, thousands of journalists are now working in the growing world of native digital news—at small non-profits like Charlottesville Tomorrow, big commercial sites like The Huffington Post and other content outlets, like BuzzFeed, that have moved into original news reporting. In a significant shift in the editorial ecosystem, most of these jobs have been created in the past half dozen years, and many have materialized within the last year alone, according to this new report on shifts in reporting power."[xxix]

There are now nearly 500 digital news outlets. While some are quite small and their hiring has not offset jobs shed by traditional firms, nearly all of these news organizations are less than 10 years old and have thus far created 5,000 new journalism jobs.[xxx]

While legacy journalists hold the majority of investigative reporting positions at digital news outlets like Pro Publica, digital natives who have never worked at traditional outlets are gaining ground and will soon dominate digital staffs.[xxxi]

No person in the history of modern journalism has enjoyed a life-long career undisrupted by changing values, methods or technologies in the study and practice of journalism. At Duquesne University, our curriculum, pedagogy and individual research agendas are joined in a rich nexus. Our goal in the classroom is to produce skilled, thoughtful and innovative multiplatform communicators who will emerge as responsible media leaders, not drones to be plugged into existing media structures. Our faculty produces scholarly papers, books and articles on Media Ethics, Media History, Media Effects, and Human-Computer Interaction that explore and problematize existing media practices and assumptions with the goal of better understanding how message creators and their publics interact – and how they might interact more constructively.

Synergy between theory and practice, combined with a willingness to adapt curriculum to respond to and anticipate cultural, technological and economic change, are the hallmarks of journalism programs that are, and will remain, viable and offer value to students – and to the publics those students will serve during their careers.

In 1922, Walter Lippmann observed that there is a "world outside" and then there are "pictures in our heads" of that world – i.e. perceptions of people and events outside of our direct experience are composed via mediation. The tragedy of the modern age, Lippmann wrote at a time when new technologies such as film and radio were overwhelming traditional modes of communication and perception, is that the two so seldom resemble one another. Citizens form perceptions – and more importantly act on those perceptions – based on what they believe to be true. And today, as in Lippmann's time, it is the journalist who employs his or her expertise, judgment and sense of responsibility to ensure the pictures in our heads accurately represent the reality we must navigate.xxxii

Even as tools and technologies change, the practice of journalism remains a vital public service with social, cultural, political and economic value. More than ever, because of the complexity of platforms employed by both content producer and content consumer, today's journalism students requires immersion in both theory and practice if they are to operate effectively as tomorrow's journalists.

Chapter 20: Intercollegiate Forensics and Mastering the Magic of Words – Professors Chad Kuyper, MFA; and Daniel Cronn-Mills, Ph.D

Chad Kuyper (MFA, Minnesota State University, Mankato, 2009) is the Director of Forensics at Florida State College at Jacksonville. Chad first came to competitive speech in 10th grade, in Owatonna, Minnesota. He would later compete in college for Minnesota State University, Mankato, where he received multiple state and national awards. He returned to Minnesota State for graduate school and coached the team as a graduate teaching assistant for three years. He became director of his own program in 2009 in Jacksonville, FL. He currently serves as the president of the Florida Intercollegiate Forensic Association, the forensics advisor to the Florida College System Activities Association, and is a member of the Executive Council of the National Forensic Association.

Dr. Daniel Cronn-Mills (Ph.D., University of Nebraska-Lincoln, 1992) is a professor in Communication Studies and a Distinguished

Faculty Scholar at Minnesota State University, Mankato. Professor Cronn-Mills is the former director of forensics at MSU, Mankato. Professor Cronn-Mills started competing in the 6th grade and continued through 7-12 grades, competed four years in college, coached as a graduate teaching assistant while in graduate school for both his master's and doctoral degrees. Professor Cronn-Mills has a storied connection with forensics in both the high school and college. Professor Cronn-Mills is a former president of the American Forensics Association and served on numerous state, regional, and national forensics committees. Professor Cronn-Mills has published more than 20 articles on forensic research. Finally, Dan has been recognized with multiple national forensic service awards, including the American Forensic Association Distinguished Service Award. Professor Cronn-Mills continues his service to forensics judging at high school and college tournaments.

Why Study Communication

You are more than likely required to take at least one course in communication at your school. And the reason is pretty straightforward. Poll after poll document communication is one of the top skillsets employers are looking for with new employees. The ability to effectively communicate with your colleagues is an important asset. The one required course is just a start to the full-range of strengths you will develop as a communication major. Studying communication will strengthen your abilities in critical thinking, problem solving, team work, and—of course—public speaking. Involvement with a forensics team is one opportunity offered by many colleges and universities to greatly improve your public speaking and public performance.

Don't let the word "forensics" confuse you. Many people think of *CSI*, *NCIS*, and *Bones* when they think of forensics. However, the word goes all the way back to the ancient Greeks. Aristotle believed forensics is one of three types of public speaking (along with deliberative and epideictic). You will learn more about Aristotle and those three types in your communication courses. For now, just remember a forensics team is competitive speech and debate (not dead bodies).

Professor Albus Dumbledore said "words are, in my not-so-humble opinion, our most inexhaustible source of magic. Capable of both inflicting injury, and remedying it" in *Harry Potter and the Deathly Hollows: Part 2* (2011). And we agree. Words can harm and words can heal. Words are magic.

You will learn the power of words and the art of magic in your communication courses. Forensics is then the opportunity to practice, practice, and practice more your magical craft of words. You will practice your spells, incantations, and potions. You will practice collecting spells (research and evidence), practice your potions (organizing your word-ingredients in the right order), and know when to swish or flick your wand (visual aids).

In the movies, we watch Harry Potter and his friends spend many hours and days practicing their magic in the Room of Requirement.* Harry coached his friends. They all helped each other get better and stronger with their magic. You will get the same opportunity with forensics. The director of your forensics program and your teammates will help you get better as you keep practicing the magic of words.

* If our Harry Potter references don't click, you really should take a weekend and binge-watch all eight movies.

"I'm Busy. Why Should I Compete in Forensics?"

Since you don't have a time-turner, let's start with an important question. Why take the time, effort, and energy to complete in inter-collegiate forensics? Forensics gives you so much. In our humble opinion, forensics is one of the best activities in college. And no matter your major, forensics will make you a better student, a better professional in your career, and a better citizen of the world.

First, obviously, your communication skills will be sharper than the average person. Time and time again, employers say they're looking for candidates with strong communication skills. Wouldn't you like to go into an interview knowing you have won actual awards for the strength of your communication? And beyond just jobs, good communicators lead better lives. Everywhere you go, you engage in communication, even if just communicating with yourself. Forensics will teach you how to communicate more effectively in all aspects of your life.

Next, your research and writing skills will grow by leaps and bounds! The kind of research forensics requires is fairly advanced. Most students report being on a forensics team makes writing and researching papers much easier. As stated in the theme of the *Bionic Man*, forensics will make you better, stronger, stronger. Professors also report forensics students in their classes often submit more sophisticated work than their classmates.

As a competitive activity, forensics will teach you the lessons of victory and defeat. After pouring your heart (and time and energy) into a speech, it's disappointing when others may do better. However, forensics teaches you how to accept defeat with grace and victory with humility. Likewise, when competing with something as personal as your own words, the thrill of victory is sweet when it arrives.

Finally, forensics give you perhaps the most important thing of all—a family. Ask people who competed in forensics and they will tell you their teammates became their best friends, a tight-knit community who provides support and companionship throughout their years in college and beyond. Forensics will become your "second family." Many team members go on to stay friends for decades after their time together in college.

Public Address is the Magic of Oratory

In public address you will research, write, and present a speech of your own (with the help of your coach, of course). From the courtroom, to the conference room; from the classroom to the work room, public address (PA) has always been a central part of effective communication. You will have the chance to compete in four different public address events.

Informative Speaking educates an audience on a subject you have carefully researched. The theme might be an exciting medical breakthrough, a technological advancement, or a fascinating social topic. Either way, you will use your powers of research, organization, and delivery to create a compelling experience for your audience.

Persuasive speaking is the opportunity to compel your audience to take action on an important social issue. Again, your research and organization skills will develop in the event. You will have the opportunity to explain to your audience about an important problem and what we can do to help make things better.

PA events may sound like papers or speeches you've already done for other classes, which is great because you're already on your way to becoming an expert. However, PA has two more events which are may be new territory for you.

After-dinner speaking is similar to informative and persuasive. You will write, research, organize, and memorize a speech with the help of a coach. But in after-dinner speaking (ADS) you must make a serious point through the use of humor. It's up to you to make your audience laugh *and* think!

Rhetorical criticism (also called communication analysis) is the fourth and final of the public-address events. In rhet crit (or CA) you analyze an interesting communication event. The event might be an important speech, an advertising campaign, a piece of art, a viral video ... anything which communicates a message to the public. Then, just like you might use a theory in English class to analyze a book or a short story, you will take a communication theory and critique the communication so the audience better understand the event. Rhet crit is, we think, the most complex of the events. But don't worry ... your coach is highly educated and will help you through the entire process. After all, coaching you is why they get paid the big bucks by the school. However, if you can master this form of competitive speaking, you will be a true forensics witch/wizard!

Limited Prep for Conjuring a Quick Spell

You will have the opportunity to compete in two fairly unique individual events on your speech team. The two events are impromptu speaking and extemporaneous speaking. Let's take a few minutes and we'll do a quick overview of the two events.

Impromptu speaking is the "speak on the fly"

event. Here's most common format. You will walk into a round, face the audience (and the judge) without an idea what you're going to talk about. The judge will hand you three quotations. You will select one of the quotations, and quickly prepare your speech. The quotations may be fairly direct ("Insanity: doing the same thing over and over again and expecting different results"—Albert Einstein) or broad ("When elephants fight, the grass gets trampled"—African proverb).

Impromptu speaking is limited to seven minutes, and the seven minutes include both preparation and presentation of the speech. You may think impromptu speaking sounds stressful. How can someone possibly develop a thesis, organize the speech into main points and sub-points, and prepare to deliver the speech in just a couple of minutes? Yikes! Don't worry, your director and coaches are highly educated and skilled individuals who help you refine your thoughts, teach you certain "tricks of the trade" for efficiently organizing your speech, and work with you in lots of practice sessions so you will be ready to rock 'n' roll when you walk into the first round of your first tournament.

Extemporaneous speaking (often just called extemp) is similar to impromptu—you will have a brief amount of time to research, organize, and prepare to present your speech. But Extemp has a few interesting differences from impromptu: First, extemp focuses on current events in the United States and the world. You will, just like impromptu, be handed three options for your speech. But the options will be three current-event questions. You will select one of the questions to answer during your speech. Here are some example extemp questions. To provide some context, we are writing this chapter will Mr. Trump, Senator Cruz, and Governor Kasich are battling to be the Republican presidential candidate, terrorist attacks have occurred throughout Europe, and some states are pushing religious-freedom bills. 1) Will the Republicans face a contested convention for selecting their nominee? 2) Should college and universities be restricting Study Abroad opportunities in Europe? 3) Can states with religious freedom laws survive th backlash from corporations?

Both impromptu and extemp have a strong connection with real-world speaking. You will be called on many times as a student and in your professional life to organize your thoughts, and gather your supporting ideas in just a few second or minutes, and then stand up and speak your mind. You will quickly find one benefit of competing in impromptu and extemp is improved efficiency when you need to write a paper for a course. Extemp and impromptu prepares you to quickly find evidence, organize your arguments, and write up your paper.

Oral Interpretation is the Magic of Stories, Poems, and Plays

One way to work your magic with speaking is to bring words to life through oral interpretation competition. Oral interpretation (oral interp) is the performing of literature. Oral interp shifts from writing a paper a short story, play, or poem to actually stepping into the world of the story/play/poem and make the character(s) inside the literature real for your audience (talk about magic!). By bringing the world of the literature to life, you understand the literature better and your audience has an incredible experience! However, oral interp is different from acting. In oral interp you don't have a stage, costumes, props, special lighting, or sound effects. Oral interp is just you and the audience. You will quickly discover forensics has five different kinds of oral interpretation events.

Prose interpretation involves you selecting a short story or a novel (your coach will help point you in the right direction to find a good a good piece), and turn it into a 10-minute performance by selecting your favorite parts and cutting out the rest. Your coach will guide you through the cutting process to trim the literature to the competitive time limit. The idea is to tell the story in a way that really pulls the audience inside the literature. You will use your voice and your body to bring the characters and story to life.

Dramatic interpretation is when you create another performance but this time, instead of using a short story or a novel, you use, well ... just about anything else. You can develop a dramatic interpretation (called DI by those in the trade) from movies, plays, podcasts—they all can work here! Then work your magic to bring the piece to life.

Two kinds of interpretation involved combining and performing multiple pieces of literature. Instead, you combine many pieces around a given theme.

Poetry interpretation combines (you guessed it) several poems into one performance. Well, you may find one really long poem. However, most competitors select many poems centering around a theme. Then, just like the other oral interpretation events, you create a dynamic performance showcasing the power and emotion in the poems you've selected.

Program oral interpretation works in almost exactly the same way, only instead of just poetry, you can pull from any genre of literature! You will usually here Program oral interpretation simply referred to as POI. You might combine part of a short story, part of a poem, something you saw on YouTube, and voilà! A POI is a captivating collage highlighting a topic or theme you feel strongly about. POI is fun because you can use and shape the literature to make an argument about a situation, an experience, an event, an emotion, or an injustice you see in the world.

The Wizarding Duels of College Debate

You will quickly learn competitive debate is nothing like what you see on TV, especially if you watch political campaign debates (and you really should be watching those campaign debates as part of being a good citizen). Anyway, let's return to collegiate debate. Depending on your school, you may have different types of debate available. "Wait a minute? Different types of debate? I thought debate was debate." Ah, padawan, you have much opportunity to learn. (Yep, we momentarily switched to *Star Wars*. Forgive our geek.) Different approaches to debate include policy debate, parliamentary debate, Lincoln-Douglas debate

(LD), public forum debate, and educational debate. We're going to cover the two most popular debate formats in the United States.

Policy debate is the oldest form of debate. Policy debate is also known as cross-examination debate, cross-x, or simply CX. Policy debate is usually two-person vs two-person, but the National Forensic Association sponsors a 1 vs 1 style called NFA-LD. The focus of policy debate is a clash between two teams presenting argument and evidence on a proposed change in policy. A debate season tends to use the same policy resolution throughout the year. Policy debate follows a fairly complex format with lots of stuff to learn.

Policy debaters have a tendency to speak very fast (and listen and write very fast). The faster a debater can talk, the more arguments and evidence they can include in the debate. All those arguments and evidence push the other side to speak just as fast (or even faster) to counter the arguments and evidence with their own arguments and evidence. All those arguments and evidence being tossed around by both sides is commonly known as speed-and-spread.

About now you may be freaking out a little bit with the complex format, lots to know, researching to find evidence and build argument, and learning talk fast (and listen and write fast). Whew ...! But don't worry, your director and teammates will guide you along the way building your skills and turning you into a top-notch debater.

The American Forensic Association-National Debate Tournament (AFA-NDT) is one of the oldest policy debate tournaments in the United States while the Cross Examination Debate Association (CEDA) hosts the largest tournament.

Parliamentary debate is the most popular debate format in the world. The debate format is based on the practices of the British House of Commons. Depending on the tournament, parliamentary debate (shortened to parli debate) is usually two-person teams but some use three-person teams. Parli debate is more fluid and dynamic than policy debate. The topic changes for each round during a tournament. Since the topic changes, you have time before each round to work with our partner planning your arguments.

Second, the research requirements for parli debate are very different than policy debate since you don't use the same resolution for the season. Parli debate is based more on common knowledge and information (but your common knowledge and information will grow while competing in this debate format).

Ok, Let's Talk Knuts, Sickles, and Galleons. What's This Going to Cost Me?

You may have some costs to participate on your school's speech or debate team. Each school has different standards for what the team pays and what the student may need to pay. Forensics can be expensive when you consider the costs including tournament registration, travel, hotel, and food (but usually the team pays for registration, travel, hotel and food).

You might need to buy a suit, blouse/shirt, tie, pumps, shoes (if you don't already own the stuff) since most speech tournaments follow "business attire." But don't let money stop you from checking out the speech and debate teams on your campus. Coaches will do everything they can to find a way for you to experience "The Greatest Show on Earth."

You will have an opportunity to participate in forensics on a state, regional and national level. Your school may belong to one or more of 17 different forensic organizations. Some focus on individual events (IE), some on various types of debate, and some cover the entire range of competitive forensics. The Council of Forensic

Organizations (COFO) provides a comprehensive listing at http://www.collegeforensics.org/. Your director will have information the organizations about the organizations for your team.

We hope you've enjoyed your brief trip through the magical halls of forensics. Now remember, to watch the skies. An owl will soon deliver your invitation to the Forensics School of Wordcraft and Wizardry. Time to practice your magic!

Reference

Barron, D., Heyman, D., & Rowling, J. K. (Producers), & Yates, D. (Director). (2011). *Harry Potter and the deathly hollows: Part 2* [motion picture]. United States: Warner Bros.

Chapter 21: Some Thoughts about Studying Communication – Professor Ronald Rice, PhD

Dr Ronald E. Rice (Ph.D., Stanford University, 1982) is the Arthur N. Rupe Chair in the Social Effects of Mass Communication, and Department Chair, in the Department of Communication, and Co-Director of the Carsey-Wolf Center, at University of California, Santa Barbara. Dr. Rice has been awarded an Honorary Doctorate from University of Montreal (2010), elected President of the ICA (2006-2007), awarded a Fulbright Award to Finland (2006), and appointed as the Wee Kim Wee Professor at the School of Communication and Information and the Visiting University Professor, both at Nanyang Technological University in Singapore (Augusts 2007-2009 and June 2010). His co-authored or (co)edited books include Organizations and unusual routines: A systems analysis of dysfunctional feedback processes (2010); Media ownership: Research and regulation (2008); The Internet and health care: Theory, research and practice (2006); Social consequences of Internet use: Access, involvement and interaction (2002); The Internet and health communication (2001); Accessing and browsing information and communication (2001); Public communication campaigns (1981, 1989, 2001, 2012); Research methods and the new media (1988); Managing organizational innovation (1987); and The new media: communication, research and technology (1984). He has published over 100 refereed journal articles and 60 book chapters. Dr. Rice has conducted research and published widely in communication science, public communication campaigns, computer-mediated communication systems, methodology, organizational and management theory, information systems, information science and bibliometrics, social uses and effects of the Internet, and social networks.

Range of the Communication Discipline

The Communication discipline covers a wide array of topics, perspectives, and philosophies, from very professional and applied (journalism, broadcasting, public speaking, rhetoric, marketing, advertising, corporate communication, web/digital design, counseling, negotiating, telecommunications design or policy, hotel/tourist management, agricultural communication, interviewing, business/management), to very academic, whether humanities or social science (media or cultural studies, education, communication science, a mix of sociology and psychology, socio-linguistics, research, public health, theory, methods), to very cognitive and biological science (cognition, bio-physiological responses, speech disorders, brain imaging, bio-social evolutionary sources and forms of human communication). Different countries and universities structure Communication in different ways, as a standalone department or several departments, or as a School or College, using a wide variety of labels (e.g., Journalism, Communication, Media Studies, Telecommunications, Radio/TV/Film, Communication and Information, Communications, etc.).

There are many communication associations around the world; their websites provide a deep and broad range of resources. See, for example:

The Association of Schools of Journalism and Mass Communication has approximately 190 member schools and departments of journalism and mass communication, most of which are located in the United States. ACEJMC accredits 109 programs in journalism and mass communications at colleges and universities in the United States (http://www.asjmc.org).

The International Communication Association (www.icahdq.org).
The National Communication Association

(www.natcom.org).

Others include American Communication
Association, Association for Business
Communication, Association of Internet
Researchers, Association of Schools of Journalism
& Mass Communication, Black College
Communication Association, Broadcast Education
Association, Central States Communication
Association, Communication Institute for Online
Scholarship, Council of Communication
Associations, Eastern Communication Association,
International Association of Business
Communicators, National Association of
Broadcasters, Public Relations Society of America,
Southern States Communication Association, and
the Western States Communication Association.
For links to these, and to world regional, and
international, communication associations, see
http://www.comm.ucsb.edu/about/national-
international.

Each of these has units representing the topical
interests of the association's members and their
research. For example, ICA
(http://www.icahdq.org/about_ica/sectioninfo.asp
) lists 25 units, such as Children, Adolescents, and
the Media; Technology; Game Studies; Health;
Intercultural; Interpersonal; Journalism Studies;

Mass; Communication; and Visual. NCA (http://www.natcom.org/interestgroups/) lists around 50, such as Argumentation and Forensics; Aging; Critical and Cultural Studies; Instructional; Nonverbal; Philosophy; Public Relations; and Theatre, Film, and New Multi-Media.

Each of the communication associations above has their own set of journals, as do other associations. Some communication journals are not related to specific associations, while many journals that publish communication research, or which communication researchers read, are formally associated with other disciplines. The Journal Citation Reports on Web of Science (available through most University libraries) lists around 70 communication journals, along with indicators of use and influence (such as citations to articles published in the journals).

Reasons for Studying Communication

Of course, any good undergraduate degree will be useful in helping students prepare for careers, through learning, training, and experience, from critical thinking to analysis to presentation and management. Liberal arts and social science courses and programs should help you to: Be skeptical about the status quo; Be curious about the natural and social world; See interconnections among what might seem separate things; Develop ethical responsibility; Not respond with fear, defensiveness or disdain about new ideas or different people; and Try to understand other perspectives.

One of the challenges with teaching and learning Communication principles is that, as everyone grows up with media and interpersonal communication, they (naturally) feel they understand everything about them (unlike studying physics, say). However, every aspect of communication has many dimensions, many possible influences and consequences, and varies across individuals, relationships, groups, communities, organizations, nations, and cultures.

Further, nearly all human activity involves, or is created/represented by and through, communication. So a better understanding of communication can help us in all contexts, and all levels, from intrapersonal health and stress, through international negotiation and diplomacy, to nonprofits, corporations and universities.

As with other fields, we develop our understandings of these processes and possible positive and negative consequences through careful and rigorous research. This may involve personal interviews (open-ended, structured), observations (in factories, at events), evaluation of documents and records (conversations, organizational memos, historical reports), focus groups (of relevant consumers or patients), surveys (local or international, print/phone/web), lab or field experiments (testing effects of a particular message or ad, identifying effects of national anti-drug campaigns), content analysis (of news stories or twitter feeds), brain imaging (assessing responses to playing violent videogames, or to persuasive environmental stories), bio-physical studies (bodily indicators of stress, eye attention, or deception), etc.

Further, communication research methods are the foundation for much of what we experience through media and in our daily lives. These include political campaign polling, viewer response to possible film endings, TV and radio ratings which are the basis for advertising revenues and advertisement placement, marketing of products, success of different organizational negotiating or strategy decisions, what are more effective and satisfying work options, under what contexts do different forms of argument work better or worse, what factors affect use and outcomes of new media, how should online and mobile device interfaces be designed, how can patients and physicians communicate more effectively, what kinds of communication help reduce what kinds of stress, etc.

More deeply, participation in, and understanding of, communication research helps one develop a deeper and more subtle understanding and awareness of what's going on in the world, a greater resistance to biased and inaccurate arguments, and a more humble assessment of human (including one's own) difficulties in achieving a reasonable, equitable, informed, and respectful communication with one's self, and with others.

Communication at the University of California, Santa Barbara

The Department of Communication at the University of California, Santa Barbara (www.comm.ucsb.edu), is part of the Division of Social Sciences in the College of Letters & Science. Teaching and research are vital activities for the Department. We offer over 65 different to more than 1200 undergraduate majors and over 25 different classes to our 35 graduate students in three core areas—interpersonal and intergroup communication, organizational communication, and media (including online and digital) studies, with many cross-cutting interests, such as health, media law, environmental communication, stereotyping, social influence, innovation, terrorism, public communication campaigns, race/ethnicity and media, etc. For a full listing of our undergraduate and graduate courses, see http://my.sa.ucsb.edu/Catalog/Current/CollegesDepartments/ls-intro/comm.aspx?DeptTab=Courses

Undergraduate students at our Department have many opportunities to participate in research with fellow students, graduate students, and faculty. These include fulfilling required research credits in all pre-major courses, being a research assistant (offered as a regular course counting toward the major), or completing a three-quarter Senior Honors Thesis. Students at UCSB have an incredibly wide array of research, internship, and travel opportunities.

Teaching Principles

I personally maintain six important teaching principles in my individual advising, undergraduate courses, and graduate courses.

Understand Student Interests

A central challenge is to find some topic, some question, or some approach that allows people to perform up to their abilities, or to find something useful or meaningful in the class. So I try to find out what interests particular students, and identify a way for them to orient assignments and projects to those interests, with a more fundamental theory, skill or awareness embedded in that project. To that end, I often provide early student surveys, using the results both as examples in class presentations, as well as guides to course content and activities.

Respect the Individual

I take each student seriously, but also the class as a whole, and the educational process in which the student and class occur. Not all students are interested in or accepting of this attention, of course; not all are prepared to be taken seriously. So they are often confronted by hard questions and high but sincere expectations when they take my classes. This particularly includes a strong emphasis on writing, showing respect for others in class, and attempting to evoke personal examples and insights during class discussions and questions.

Use Media Materials when Appropriate

I use different media when they are appropriate and develop materials that will visually and aurally help to explain a complex problem. For example, my classes utilize live Internet sites, YouTube videos, online case studies and publications, whiteboard text and diagrams, computer simulations, student presentations, student debates, handouts, discussions, lectures, tutorials, question-sessions, and cross-student critiques.

Emphasize Student Experience and Contributions

Especially in undergraduate Internet courses, but also in specialized graduate courses, there are many experts in any class, so I design my courses around each quarter's participants, using their knowledge and experience to make the material richer for the other students. The students realize that only some of what they can learn comes from the teacher, so their university experience is enriched by their classmates, and, when possible, by projects outside of the university.

Treat Students as Colleagues

I have personally seen students who have flourished and made original contributions when they realized that the outcome really was their responsibility and their product, when I really did place my trust in their judgment. This achievement seems to me to be much more relevant to education than having them crank out one paper for a faculty member. I provide graduate TAs to present case studies, course content, or course lectures.

Be Organized and Professional

It is importantly professionally, and for the sake of students' uncertainty levels, to be well-organized, explicit, on time, and accessible. My reading packets or online course materials are always completed well before the course begins. My syllabi and online courses contain every detail about the course, grading, readings, and assignments all in one place, with tables of contents and schedules and discussion notes. I respond immediately to any questions or suggestions about the printed or online content of courses.

Possible Communication Careers

Communication, because of its wide range of topics, provides a foundation for many careers. Here are just a few

(http://www.comm.ucsb.edu/undergrad/career/comm-careers). Also see NCA's Career Resources at

http://www.natcom.org/CommunicationCareerPaths/.

Actor	Film Director	Press Secretary
Advertising Copywriter	Film Producer	Producer
Announcer	Film Tape Librarian	Product Promotion
Associate Publisher	Floor Manager	Production Editor
Audience Analyst	Foreign Relations Officer	Public Administrator
Blog, Social Media, Website Manager	Fundraiser	Public Affairs Director
Book Designer	Human Resources Specialist	Public Information Officer
Broadcast Station Mgr.	Human Rights Officer	Public Opinion Researcher
Campaign Director		Public Relations Manager
Communication Trainer	Labor Relations Specialist	Publications Advisor
Community Relations Director	Lobbyist	Publicity Manager
Community Relations Liaison	Market Analyst	Reporter
Consumer Advocate	Marketing Specialist	Research and Editorial Specialist
Corporate Public Affairs Specialist	Media Analyst	Sales Representative
Counselor	Media Buyer	Speech Instructor
Creative Director	Media Planner	Social Media Analyst
Customer Relations Representative	Media Relations Manager	Staff Consultant
Director of Corporate	Mediator	Technical Director
	Mgr., Investor	Technical Writer

Communication	Relations	Trainer
Disc Jockey	News Anchor	Transmitter Engineer
Editorial Director	News Director	Web designer
Educator	News Supervisor	Writer
Event Planner		

Thank You From the Publisher

Thank you readers/students for downloading and reading this book. We would also like to thank all the chapter authors/co-authors for their contributions and support to this initiative to help the student community.

If you, the readers/students, liked this book, we would be very grateful if you could leave your honest review as to how this book benefited you (one short sentence would be fine). Please visit Amazon (http://bit.ly/communicationmajor) or any other retailer's platform to leave your review.

Please visit www.amazon.com/author/college for the list of other books published by the Curious Academic Publishing.

If you have any suggestions/feedback or questions about this book, please let us know by emailing us at curious.publishing@gmail.com. If your institution/organization needs bulk copies of the print edition of the book at discounted price or the hardcover copy of the Interdisciplinary Encyclopedia of Arts & Humanities Majors, please contact us.

The Curious Academic Publishing Team

Other Books from the Curious Academic Publishing

Note: Search your books on Amazon with the key words (e.g. Accounting + Curious).

1. Accounting for the UNDECIDED Students, Their Major & Career Advisors, and Parents: Why Study Accounting (http://bit.ly/accounting_major)

2. Advertising (http://bit.ly/advertising-major)

3. Agriculture (http://bit.ly/myagri)

4. Biology (http://bit.ly/biology-major)

5. Business Management (http://bit.ly/business-major)

6. Buddhist Studies (http://bit.ly/ourbuddha)

7. Celebrity (http://bit.ly/mycelebrity)

8. Chemical Engineering (http://bit.ly/chemicaleng)

9. Chemistry (http://bit.ly/chemistrymajor)

10. Christianity (http://bit.ly/christianitymajor)

11. Civil Engineering (http://bit.ly/myceng)

12. Computer Science

   (http://bit.ly/mycomputerscience)

13. Criminology (http://bit.ly/criminaljusticemajor)

14. Environmental-Science (http://bit.ly/whyenvironment)

15. Entrepreneurship (http://bit.ly/whyentrepreneurship

16. Economics (http://bit.ly/economicsmajor)

17. Electrical Engineering (http://bit.ly/e-engineering)

18. Exercise and sports (http://bit.ly/exercise-sport)

19. Fashion design

   (http://bit.ly/whyfashiondesign)

20. Finance (http://bit.ly/whyfashiondesign)

21. Food science (http://bit.ly/myfoodscience)

22. Forestry (http://bit.ly/myforestry)

23. Geology (http://bit.ly/geologymajor)

24. Geography (http://bit.ly/mygeography)

25. Graphic Design (http://bit.ly/mygraphicdesign)

26. Health Informatics

(http://bit.ly/myhealthinformatics)

27. History (http://bit.ly/historymajor)

28. Hotel & Hospitality (http://bit.ly/hotel-hospitality)

29. Human Resource Management

(http://bit.ly/hrm-major)

30. Information Systems and Technology (http://bit.ly/informationsystems)

31. Internet Marketing (http://bit.ly/internet-marketing-major)

32. Interior Design (http://bit.ly/myinteriordesign)

33. International Business

(http://bit.ly/myinternational-business)

34. International Relations (http://bit.ly/my-international-relations)

35. Journalism (http://bit.ly/myjournalism)

36. Law (http://bit.ly/whylaw)

37. Legal studies (http://bit.ly/mylegalstudies)

38. Mechanical engineering

39. (http://bit.ly/mechanicalengineering)
Marketing (http://bit.ly/marketing-paperback)

40. Materials science (http://bit.ly/materialseng)

41. Mathematics (http://bit.ly/majormath)

42. Medical Science

(http://bit.ly/mymedicalscience)

43. MBA (http://bit.ly/yesmba)

44. Nutrition and weight management
(http://bit.ly/nutrition-weight)

45. Nursing (http://bit.ly/nursing-major)

46. Pathology (http://bit.ly/mypathology)

47. Petroleum engineering (http://bit.ly/petroeng)

48. Pharmacy (http://bit.ly/pharmacymajor)

49. Philosophy (http://bit.ly/philosophymajor)

50. Physiology (http://bit.ly/physiologymajor)

51. Physics (http://bit.ly/physicsmajor)

52. Political Science

(http://bit.ly/mypoliticalscience)

53. Procurement (http://bit.ly/myprocurement)

54. Program Evaluation (http://bit.ly/program-evaluation)

55. Psychology (http://bit.ly/why-psychology)

56. Public Policy (http://bit.ly/studypolicy)

57. Public speaking (http://bit.ly/mypublicspeaking)

58. Public Health (http://bit.ly/ourpublichealth)

59. Real estate (http://bit.ly/studyrealestate)

60. Romance (http://bit.ly/myromance)

61. Sociology (http://bit.ly/majorsociology)

62. Sexology (http://bit.ly/studysex)

63. Social media (http://bit.ly/mediamajor)

64. Statistics (http://bit.ly/mystatistics)

65. Supply chain (http://bit.ly/studyscm)

66. Teacher Education

67. Travel & tourism (http://bit.ly/tourism-travel)

68. Writing (http://bit.ly/writingmajor)

End Notes

---

[i] According to several credible source: http://www.bls.gov/emp/ joboutlook. The **Job Outlook** survey is a forecast of **employers'** intentions to hire new college graduates.

[ii] *Lambda Pi Eta* is the official Communication Studies honor society of the National Communication Association (NCA).

[iii] The McNair Scholars Program prepares qualified undergraduates for entrance to a PhD program in all fields of study. The goals of the program are to increase the number of first-generation, low-income and/or underrepresented students in PhD programs, and ultimately, to diversify the faculty in colleges and universities across the country.

[iv] The College Assistance Migrant Program (CAMP) assists students who are migratory or seasonal farmworkers (or children of such workers) enrolled in their first year of undergraduate studies at an IHE. The funding supports completion of the first year of studies. Competitive five-year grants for CAMP projects are made to IHEs or to nonprofit private agencies that cooperate with such institutions. The program serves approximately 2,000 CAMP participants annually.

[v] Susan Adams (Oct. 11, 2013) http://www.forbes.com/sites/susanadams/2013/10/11/the-10-skills-employers-most-want-in-20-something-employees/

[vi] Reinsch, N. L. Jr., Gardner, J. A. (2014). Do communication abilities affect promotion decisions? Some data from the c-suite. *Journal of Business and Technical Communication, 28,* 31-57.

[vii] Susan Adams (Oct. 11, 2013) http://www.forbes.com/sites/susanadams/2013/10/11/the-10-skills-employers-most-want-in-20-something-employees/

[viii] Aristotle, *The Nicomachean ethics*, Trans. A.K. Thomas (1953). New York: Penguin.

[ix] Robert F. Kennedy. "Remarks on the Assassination of Martin Luther King, Jr." April 4, 1968. Indianapolis, IN. http://www.americanrhetoric.com/speeches/rfkonmlkdeath.html.

[x] "What is Communication?" National Communication Association. http://www.natcom.org/discipline/.

[xi] "Top 10 College Majors." *The Princeton Review*. 2014. http://www.princetonreview.com/college/top-ten-majors.aspx.

[xii] Susan Adams. "The 10 Skills Employers Most Want in 20-Seomthing Employees." Forbes.com. October 11, 2013. www.forbes.com.

[xiii] Christy Clark. "In-Demand Degrees to Start in 2013. *Yahoo! Education*. http://education.yahoo.net/articles/in_demand_degrees_in_2013.htm.

[xiv] Terence Loose. "Best and Worst Degrees for Employment. *Yahoo! Education*. http://education.yahoo.net/articles/best_and_worst_degrees.htm.

[xv] You can watch the interview, currently posted to YouTube, at https://www.youtube.com/watch?v=tpgcEYpLzP0.

[xvi] National Communication Association. *Pathways to Communication Careers in the 21st Century*. https://www.natcom.org/ProductCatalog/Product.aspx?id=984.

[xvii] To learn more about the Department of Communication Studies at IUPUI, visit us here: http://liberalarts.iupui.edu/comm/.

[xviii] Chris Young, a 2007 Duquesne JMA graduate, is an associate reporter at CPI and his work has appeared in a variety of prestigious national news venues.

[xix] Gee, Auger and Tanes-Ehle, "Audience Assessment of the Quality. Usability and Trustworthiness of News Content Created and Delivered Via Mobile Devices,"

http://www.duq.edu/academics/schools/liberal-arts/academic-departments-of-liberal-arts/journalism-and-multimedia-arts/research (accessed 5/13/2014).

xx Our program does not offer graduate scholarships, however we offer 12 assistantships per year – these pay a student's tuition and provide a modest stipend in return for research and teaching assistance within the department. Last year we were also host to a Fullbright Scholar.

xxi Mitchell, Amy, et. al. Pew Research Center's Project for Excellence in Journalism: Digital: As Mobile Grows Rapidly, the Pressures on News Intensify. http://stateofthemedia.org/2013/digital-as-mobile-grows-rapidly-the-pressures-on-news-intensify/

xxii I currently have a book proposal on digital media ethics out for review.

xxiii The online iteration of the *Off the Bluff* magazine can be found at: offthebluff.com

xxiv A student documentary on the decline of a steel town, and many other examples of student work in journalism and other areas can be found at: http://www.duquesnemultimedia.com/

xxv Schmidt, Eric and Cohen, Jared, *The New Digital Age: Transforming Nations, Businesses and Our Lives*. New York: Vintage Book, 2014.

xxvi Finberg, Howard, "Journalism Needs the Right Skills to Survive," Poynter, April 9, 2014. http://www.poynter.org/how-tos/journalism-education/246563/journalism-needs-the-right-skills-to-survive/ (accessed April 24, 2014).

xxvii Steiger, Paul, A Closer Look: Three Golden Ages of Journalism?" Pro Publica, Feb. 7, 2014. http://www.propublica.org/article/a-closer-look-three-golden-ages-of-journalism (accessed May 13, 2014).

xxviii Briggs, Mark. *Journalism Next.* Los Angles: CQ Press, 2013, p. 1.

xxix Jurkowitz, Mark, "The Growth in Digital News Reporting: What it Means for Journalism and News Consumers. Pew Foundation, March 26, 2014. http://www.journalism.org/2014/03/26/the-growth-in-digital-reporting/ (accessed May 20, 2014.)

xxx Pew Research Journalism Project. "State of the News Media 2014," Pew Foundation, March 26, 2014. http://www.journalism.org/2014/03/26/the-growth-in-digital-reporting/ (accessed April 22, 2014).

xxxi ibid.
xxxii Lippmann, Walter. *Public Opinion.*   New York, Harcourt,
Brace, 1922, p. 29.

www.ingramcontent.com/pod-product-compliance
Lightning Source LLC
Chambersburg PA
CBHW020830210326
41598CB00019B/1852